I AM I

The Indweller of Your Heart

BOOK THREE

Also by David Knight

Pathway

Deliverance of Love, Light and Truth

I am I: The Indweller of Your Heart—Book One

I am I: The Indweller of Your Heart—Book Two

I am I: The Indweller of Your Heart—'Collection'

Leave the Body Behind—Sojourns of the Soul

A Pocket Full of God

I AM I

The Indweller of Your Heart

BOOK THREE

52 LESSONS TO HELP YOU REAP YOUR OWN ETERNAL HARVEST

David Knight

I AM I The Indweller of Your Heart—Book Three

Copyright © 2013 by DPK Publishing—AscensionForYou.

Previous ISBN—13: 978-0-9926882-0-2
This edition—ISBN: 978-1-8380091-8-2
       eISBN: 978-1-914936-09-8

Updated Version:
Copyright © 2021 DPK Publishing—AscensionForYou.

Printed in the United States of America.

All rights reserved and the moral right of the Author has been asserted. Without limiting the rights under copyright reserved above, no part of this publication may be reproduced, stored in or introduced into a retrieval system, or transmitted, in any form, or by any means (electronic, mechanical, photocopying, recording, or otherwise) without the prior written permission of both the copyright owner and the above publisher of this book.

A CIP catalogue record for this book is available from the British library.

2021 Cover layout/design by Nathan Dasco

For further information contact David via his website/blog:
https://www.AscensionForYou.com

If you enjoy reading *I AM I The Indweller of Your Heart*—Book Three—you can find further inspiring and motivation books when you join David's mission for a 'full and blissful life'.

To learn more, visit www.AscensionForYou.com
and download *Deliverance of Love, Light and Truth* for free.

ACKNOWLEDGMENTS

To God, for the privilege bestowed upon me, in receiving these words of wisdom, knowledge and peace ... for this book has created yet another steppingstone towards the eternal love and bliss which is within us all.

To all guides and teachers from within God's light hierarchy, who have truly given and shared their love so freely, making my life (and heart) so rich and complete, that mere words cannot begin to describe how I feel.

I wish to thank my wife Caroline in recognition of her support, patience and love, Rachael Hardcastle and Nathan Dasco, for their creativity and for the encouragement of all past and present members of the Peterborough Sai Baba group ... and my family and friends who are so special to me too.

MAY GOD BLESS YOU ALL

TABLE OF CONTENTS

FOREWORD..11

LESSON 1:
THE WINDOW..12

LESSON 2:
BREATHE..15

LESSON 3:
ONE..18

LESSON 4:
DIARY..21

LESSON 5:
REMORSE...24

LESSON 6:
SURROUNDINGS...27

LESSON 7:
THE MEADOW...30

LESSON 8:
NUTS AND BOLTS..34

LESSON 9:
CLARITY..37

LESSON 10:
EVERYTHING..40

LESSON 11:
QUEST...43

LESSON 12:
PATHWAYS

LESSON 13: OCEANS	49
LESSON 14: PURITY	53
LESSON 15: FACT OR FICTION	56
LESSON 16: CALLING	60
LESSON 17: TEST	63
LESSON 18: CLOTHES	67
LESSON 19: CAMOUFLAGE	70
LESSON 20: PORTAL	73
LESSON 21: CONFERENCE	76
LESSON 22: WHISPERS	82
LESSON 23: STRUCTURE	85
LESSON 24: LIFE—PATH	88
LESSON 25: LAZY DAYS?	91
LESSON 26: UNKNOWN	94

- LESSON 27: CONTINUITY 97
- LESSON 28: HOLLOW 100
- LESSON 29: SLAVE 103
- LESSON 30: FIELDS OF GOLD 106
- LESSON 31: IMAGINE 109
- LESSON 32: HURTING 112
- LESSON 33: SOMETIMES 115
- LESSON 34: LONGING 118
- LESSON 35: SERVICE 121
- LESSON 36: FOG 124
- LESSON 37: BURN 127
- LESSON 38: SHIPS 130
- LESSON 39: HOLDING ON 133
- LESSON 40: RHYTHM 136

LESSON 41:
SUSTENANCE..139
LESSON 42:
SERENITY...142
LESSON 43:
ELEVATED...145
LESSON 44:
WAITING?..148
LESSON 45:
BLESSED..151
LESSON 46:
KEEPER..154
LESSON 47:
THE RETURN...157
LESSON 48:
FOCUS..160
LESSON 49:
TIME...163
LESSON 50:
PURIFICATION..166
LESSON 51:
PROPHECY..169
LESSON 52:
WELCOME...172
CONCLUSION..175
FURTHER READING...176
ABOUT THE AUTHOR..178
INVITATION FROM DAVID KNIGHT..........................179

FOREWORD

This may be the first time that you have set eyes upon these lessons and inner dictations. Or, if you have read—or heard—books one and two before, you will be familiar with how and why these words have fallen upon each page.

You read them now because I meant you to. This is the right time in your own spiritual development to live and become 'realised'. Your efforts will help you reap your own eternal harvest.

I trust that deep within your heart, you'll be reminded you are love and light. Remember, you are immensely powerful and brilliant, and majestic. In fact, so much so that you're able to move forward to experience and display your own divinity for others to sense and feel and share, too.

Then, having received new knowledge—and through your own life experiences—you will gain wisdom. And with this wisdom, you can truly shine and resonate with positive thoughts and words and deeds.

I hope your continuing journey of self-realisation is full of joy and hope, with dreams fulfilled. Comprehend too that you—and every living thing that exists—are all part of creation.

Therefore, while you learn—or re-learn this by 'remembering'—with the aid of these lessons, you will live and share the life in which you always wanted to create ... not only for yourself, but for others, too.

LESSON 1:

THE WINDOW

Wherever you are, and however old you may think or deem yourself to be, know that I will forever welcome you to sense and feel the love of my heart. So, if you were to pause and reflect upon these words, you'll realise I am your experience, and you also become mine. We are 'one'; whole, complete, and free.

For many days, weeks, months or even years, you may not have felt this way. It was as if you believed you're trapped, as if by circumstance or fate, forbidding entry to—or of—something beautiful and new within your life. Understand there is no time limit. There is no lock, which cannot be turned. Therefore, just remember, your heart is the key to opening all the right doors in every aspect of work and rest and play.

With every decision one makes, do not feel 'fate' has previously dictated what you have said, thought or carried out, but simply try—right now—to stop controlling the so-called inevitable. Just go with the flow. Please understand ... I constantly witness the pushing and shoving in so many lives ... all the while people try to manipulate and shape an outcome—to bend it to one's own will and desire. Instead (as mentioned in numerous texts over the eons of time), give yourself a moment to pause and reflect. Become calm. Then progress—with every step—knowing that all is as it should be.

It is only fear that inhibits and endeavours to restrict you into making rash and spontaneous decisions, which not only affect yourself, but those you feel matter most around you. With fear, one constantly feels that doors are shut. Or that the window of opportunity has been closed, suggesting a missed chance to view and experience pastures new.

Consider for a moment a map. Perhaps it's a town or city or country, or even of the world. If you were to close your eyes and place your finger upon it, you could then pretend it is your next destination, as if you were planning to take a holiday. Therein lies many questions. 'How do I get there? What is the fastest or most scenic route to take? Is there a safer passage? And how much will it cost?'

With all these decisions to face, your preparations must be complete to make a successful journey in reaching your goal. So much time and effort is placed upon it, whether for a weekend away, or that week or fortnight of fun in the sun.

Now try to contemplate upon your soul's journey and true essence, as only you can decide how important—if at all—it is. Remember, you are not a body with a soul, but you are divinity, as if held within a precious shell; an outer garment that enables you to think, feel, and breathe upon the impermanent world in which you currently live.

So, do you make any effort to establish who and what you truly are? Has the mind stifled the inquiring heart, placing the true goal of self-realization into bliss and peace upon the back burner? Are you waiting for the window to be opened for you? Is there some precise and magical time—without a need to think for oneself—to state, 'Oh come on dear God … is that really such a crime?'

Well, know that I do not convey these messages and lessons to chastise, condemn, ridicule, or frustrate you. Truth cannot do this. Only one's own self-doubt and confusion can try to lead you further away from me … indeed, further than what you think, or believe that you already are. No, for I am nearer than near … like the blood running through your veins—and the conscience that pricks your mind—after thought and word and deeds have materialized.

So, we are not separated. We are eternally linked, as light throughout all space, time, and dimension. Understand that if separation and division were true, the wave would not merge with the ocean. Rain would not fall from the clouds … and the night could never follow day.

You, too, are all entwined and connected like threads woven together to form the truth. But without the structure of love, you would cease to exist as you do, as soul, body, and mind. Like a jumper without a hole for your head, a necklace with a missing link, and a plane without a wing, nothing would function and be a worthwhile expression of creation. However, because you are divine …no matter your colour, shape, and size, or even if you feel incomplete or different, you are always—and forever will be— 'whole'.

Therefore, I ask whether you can believe this. If you do, you can also believe in yourself, and hence me. With belief and trust, nothing can prevent or deny the truth, rising within the well of your heart. Your thirst for sustenance and truth will always be quenched—and never denied—because inside you is every answer you could ever seek or wish for.

Know that you are a living flame, a spark of divinity which shines as brightly as you could ever desire to be. That is the true reflection and reality —the 'I AM I'—and as such, each day can be a new beginning. So, forget and do not waste time on the past. You can then use every moment as an opportunity to shine on who and what you are and can also yet become.

By expanding your love far beyond the walls where you live and work and yearn to be, friendships are formed. Then people, cities, and nations can blossom together, to radiate and exude the fragrance of love and peace across the world.

I will cast it upon—and by—the wind, which is my breath, so the nectar of my being will flourish upon the fertile soil (soul), and within all hearts. Tears of joy and rays of hope from the sun (Son) will nourish and sustain all who partake in truth. Weeds of deceit, hate, anguish, and pain will become eradicated through determination and perseverance and fortitude and faith.

This is my promise to one and all. I will not close the window ... because the window is only of the mind's making. Indeed, the road that you travel is clearly marked ahead. When you control the senses, the mind, body, and soul are in unison—seeing and seeking as one.

So, now push aside the doubts and fears because the opportunity knocks for one and all. Take it. Grasp it. For you truly belong in my heart ... and 'I' am forever within yours. Amen.

LESSON 2:
BREATHE

Welcome once again to all souls ... both new and old! As you sit and read this text, listening to these words being spoken aloud, or perhaps even understanding their meaning through the touch of your hands, I ask whether they flow more easily through you.

Appreciate that when you have an open heart and mind, love, and light travel unrestricted through the ether and all dimensions of time and space. However, without compassion and with a lack of understanding and trust for oneself—and me—knowledge and wisdom, becomes hindered, distorted, and shallow. One could compare this with a garment so tightly worn around your chest that merely breathing becomes laboured or even painful.

In this scenario, one would no doubt ache to breathe more clearly again. Can you imagine the relief of breathing freely, with ease, and without pain? You may well know of someone who needs medical aid to do this. Or having to use ventilators or oxygen cylinders just to survive. This restricts a body as if held in a vice-like grip. One may even question whether they are indeed 'free' at all. Remember, it is vitally important to never fall into the depths of despair. It can never tie your heart and true love down, held captive, become broken or even diluted by time or distance.

So, how are you feeling right now, within your body, soul, or mind? Happy and glad? Or do you feel dissatisfied and even frustrated by family, friends, your home, or work? What forces seemingly restrict your capacity to just be yourself by being true to you? Do you imagine you are suffocating under another's pressure by thought, word, or deed? Or perhaps your body currently makes you seem tired, worn, or burnt out inside? If so, stop. Yes, stop right here, right now!

In such times, you only need to know—and also keep reminding yourself —you have been living as an individual. You are attempting to divide and separate oneself, when in fact you are a vital part or cog within the wheel of society. However, do not concern yourself with how important a role you think you play upon this stage called 'life.' You do not need to be the main character, who apparently takes all the plaudits and congratulations.

You just need to understand that whatever the position or part—however minor or major it seems to be—whether you are working for yourself, helping with voluntary or charitable work, or running a multi-national company or business, every single person can contribute to the well-being and welfare of humanity.

Do not believe self-worth is judged by your income or status? Know that those who lie in poverty and destitution may shine hearts of gold, perhaps as old souls, who—if they're seen—make one's own needs and worries pale in comparison. Realise too, only by living in truth, with kindness, forgiveness, righteousness, love, non-attachment—and each day emanating positive thoughts—can your aims and aspirations become fulfilled.

One is only ever restricted by fear. This is self-induced or reflected upon you by another. Perhaps by someone close, or even those totally disconnected, like those who are (seemingly) in authority over state and country.

Understand, too, that those weeds of despair, anxiety—and fear—which attempt to grow and strangle the purity of truth that flows from above and below can suffocate the individual and the masses. Just like your garden weeds, they are tenacious; continually appearing year after year, season after season. Therefore, you can only overcome them by constantly being vigilant, preventing the smallest hint of ego and self-centred preservation from taking hold, stopping you from fulfilling your true potential and goal of self-realization.

With hearts and hands combined, villages, towns, cities, and nations can become unified and prosper. By cultivating those seeds of love through right action, hearts and minds can grow strong. They withstand any winters of discontent to rise into the sun—and Son.

Try not to let the years go by, with life often feeling as if it is on autopilot. Instead, acknowledge it is yourself, for only you can once again take control of your destiny, fulfilling your own wishes and dreams. The real question to ask is whether you are currently satisfied, and if you are truly content or not. I do not mean with the material possessions around you, but to recognize whether you feel fulfilled. With this, you can only be honest with yourself, as no one else can answer it for you.

In contrast to overcoming any adversities or times when you think you are painfully restricted, could you ever believe that there may be instances, or reasons, when struggling to breathe might be because of something positive? For example, when two hearts and souls connect—in truth—together?

Indeed, when one realises, they have fallen in love, and merely being in their partner's presence, or even more so—by an enforced absence from their smile, embrace, or kiss—can all become those moments when your breath is taken away. There is a deep and burning desire which is so strong, it feels as if you may drown in your own vacuum of tears. Any separation stops you from functioning. It is so overwhelming that one may feel they would rather die. Is this too extreme? Is this a lie? If that was the case, just ask those who fall upon their knees to pray or curl up under covers and cry.

Now then, imagine our love for each other—yes, you and I—is stronger than even this single moment since time immemorial. How can this be? And how could I ever condone or create such a scenario? Well, believe me when I say that I haven't, because although the love connection is true and eternal, the separation is false. Know that light-years in distance and time are irrelevant to me. The seeds of truth—scattered throughout creation—are from, through, and to me. There can be no division.

It is only in the physical embodiment that you feel unconnected from each other and me. This is simply because memories of the mind try to enforce their will over the feelings and reality of the heart. This, with your soul's karma, has been built up over many lifetimes in order to experience and grow, and to share and shine the brilliance of your light and love. Therefore, you must now scratch deep below the surface to reveal your reality.

Appreciate, too, that there are many who falsely believe in secret codes and hidden biblical treasures, which must be unearthed in order to progress or even 'ascend'. This is not so, as all you could ever wish for and need is right there inside of you. Remember, you are divine, a spark of my divinity, and a living flame of love and light.

So then, feel me as the wind, simply blowing across your face, but also know me as the universe and all creation … forever growing and expanding beyond 'mind' and your dreams. Understand that the life force and energy flows through my beating heart into every fibre, particle, atom, and all elements known or unknown to the human race … when I 'breathe'. Amen.

LESSON 3:

ONE

I welcome you to feel and share from the well of truth, for deep within, peace reigns inside every element of life. Then, having acknowledged this, there can be an increase of understanding and belief, both of yourself and of me—I AM I—because we are 'one'.

I have continually stated that there is no division or separateness throughout creation. So, there can only be one religion which emanates from all souls—called 'love'. There can only be a single universal language readily understood and comprehended by all of existence ... and it is the same love which comes from, through, and to the heart.

Therefore, as you rise from your bed—whether morning, noon, or night—what do you feel or think of? Do you have a false fear, or a very real fright? I ask, because when you wake, try to appreciate each day. Know it gives you the opportunity to shine and achieve important things. I do not mean that you're suddenly going to invent something unique, but what you can do is create a new, true beginning, not only for yourself but also for those nearby and far beyond the walls of your home.

Indeed, throughout your busy life, if you could only find the time to pause and hear me—if only for a few seconds—it would be so much easier for you to believe. For example, if you were in a forest, you would sense the whispers of my voice amongst the leaves of trees. If you were upon hills or mountains, I state you could then feel the vibrations and echoes of many tears, shed over the eons of time, during many cycles of rebirth and death.

Perhaps you can do this, or maybe you cannot. Nonetheless, we are where we are. So, by reflecting upon the peace and stillness, you will become accustomed to knowing and understanding the truth which lies in your heart. Comprehend too, that just like the blood, which is pumped around your body and veins, love flows through the actions, words, and thoughts which emanate from both your heart and head.

However, please appreciate that love, when enforced, cajoled, or manipulated, is weak. It dissipates and remains wafer thin. And, just like thin ice, any stress or pressure between two hearts can cause it to crack and splinter. This creates holes not so easily repaired—unless patience, forgiveness, and compassion take hold. In contrast, unconditional love is understood and felt over great distances. It stays truthful. It can withstand both tests of time and travel, across—and to—many dimensions of energy.

I will always reiterate these things to you. True love can withstand the weight of life's 'ups and downs'—together with those burdens of your past choices—to support you. Thus, one grows in confidence. You not only keep positive to help you achieve your goals and aims, but in the sense that you can comprehend something far greater than that of your physical presence which exists.

So, when you walk in truth, you do not need to fear where you place your feet. The pathway across the emotional waters of your existence remains strong and enhanced. This leads you onwards and forwards to eternal bliss and peace. Where you place your feet, your kindness will grip and gently help you. Indeed, by taking one step at a time—to cross over those pools of emotions with dry eyes—there's no outpouring of ego or tears, which are fuelled by frustrations, anxiety, or fears.

Then, as days, weeks, months, and years roll by, you can also reflect. You can look back, not with any regrets, but knowing that the choices you had made were honest. They carried integrity, hope, and real passion to serve as a valued member of society. In fact, life is so very much about service, not for the self where selfishness reigns, but in those selfless actions which help promote unity. This link's hands of friendship with family, colleagues, and neighbours into one unbroken chain of harmony, peace, and love.

Looking forward now, try not to despair. Though do not forget the troubles which seem to knock upon another's door, across the cities or nations of the world. Remember, what is occurring in many countries is the tide of discontent amongst 'ordinary' people. Such civilizations no longer wish to live under dictatorship and hardship, and from the suppressed idolization of demonic leaderships.

Some may feel these are harsh word. They can also mean nothing at all, merely letters on a piece of paper. However, to those without food, water, clothes, or shoes—and who live in a regime without democracy and freedom of choice—I hope you understand that eventually those barriers of fear and pain, (which are attempting to crush and hold hearts and hands bound in age old doctrines) will come crashing down under the weight of a tsunami of tears. Yes, those same tears released through love and light will well up and flood. They will disperse evil, while hearts of truth will live and breathe fresh air once more.

Indeed, the world may seem a big place, but because of your earthbound technology there is little hiding place for dark shadows to hide. The so-called common man, woman, and child will one day bask in the freedom of the sunlight to forge a clearer, brighter world. All will realise that starvation, cruelty, and persecution must become a thing of the past.

When each soul sees the same God, which lives in themselves—also lies in the heart of another—then the heavens will open. Crystallized tears of divine love will cascade like fountains of pure and clear light in all directions. Never doubt this but continue to unite under the banner of your heart. Then, the world community can hear, see, and help those overcome pain and disharmony, bringing relief for body, mind, and soul. One day, all of humankind's anguish will fade. Hopes and dreams will become fulfilled with sincerity and peace for one and all.

In reality, you might not currently live within a war-torn country, suffering deprivation and starvation, or in immense hardship. Therefore, some might just say, 'to thank their lucky stars', as it is so easy to forget your brother, sister, friend, or stranger across the other side of the world. One may flick the light switch or turn the central heating on, lay their head upon a soft pillow, have shoes upon their feet, money in their pockets, wear a coat upon their back, have food and water in their stomach—yet still they remain dissatisfied. Please understand this is not a guilt trip, to be self-induced or forced upon the reader, but to remind you of contentment, attachment, and gratitude.

Some will say that to have good health is the real or true wealth, but having an open heart which can forgive, share, serve, and support any other being, animal, person, or soul is of a greater importance. In fact, you then have my grace in abundance. Please understand, just one blessing of my grace is beyond all known and unknown, so-called riches in existence. Therefore, with love, you are everything ... and everything is you. And you recognize and know that we are truly 'one'.

However, without love, the heart shrivels and shrinks. It resembles a tiny nut inside its shell—so much so that barely any light emanates from 'within'. One can drift throughout time, without purpose and forever doubting.

Appreciate right now that I will guide you all away from such an outcome. So please trust in yourselves and trust the goodness of your hearts to shine the true brilliance which you behold. Wish, dream, and pray for it. The world cannot fail to respond when love flows from, through, and to all hearts. Amen.

LESSON 4:
DIARY

Once again, I welcome all souls and hearts. May they bear witness and read or feel these words which flow like whispers, cast upon the ether as my voice and breath.

Know that whether through the 'inner voice', or via visions, visitations, prophets, and the avatars throughout creation, many civilizations across many worlds have recorded their sacred texts. They are handed down for generations upon generations to live, learn, and remember who and what they truly are.

However, when all life has attained self-realization, every soul will comprehend that even the akashic records—which hold all the written 'works' of wisdom since the dawn of time—and held within the heavenly realms of light, will become obsolete. This is because you become soul centred and not self-centred, and every level and vibration of love and energy through and to and from my heart is acknowledged and totally understood. There will be no form of 'life' who cannot comprehend they are 'one', a divine spark of an eternal flame of truth.

For now, there are many who have inner fears. Like personal secrets or hidden desires, they deeply wish for them to remain 'unknown'—by being disguised—which is like writing in invisible ink into a diary. Therefore, if you believe each page represents a day of your own embodiment, how much love and light inside your heart can you truthfully and freely display? What is it within your life you can change? What can you reveal to those who know, or don't even know, you?

Are you keeping your true feelings and thoughts of your heart close to your chest like a closed book? Or are you now at the point and stage of your life where you not only sense, but realise deep inside, it's time for the true essence of your soul to shine?

Please remember you have a golden heart. This is so precious that no earthly jewel can compare. The core of your being radiates like thousands or billions of suns, and therefore, your love and light cannot be contained. No feelings of truth can be boxed or stored away. How else could loved one's sense and feel your thoughts as they connect across the other side of the world—and of course so much further than this—through the numerous dimensions of time and space too?

That said, even though all souls are connected, do you currently have no cares in the world? Or do you truly—and simply—not care for the world in which you live? Is the responsibility to share love and peace shared by the many, or do they find they cannot—or will not—share in life and be as one? These are direct and forthright analogies and questions which all souls should consider. I state these points because I do not want you to continue feeling that you cannot make a difference ... because you can.

Foremost, one can start by tending to the 'garden' of virtues I have previously mentioned. Indeed, if you attended to them daily, those weeds of doubt, frustration, and fear will be eradicated over time. Through your own efforts to sow the seeds of love, compassion, right-conduct, truth, and peace, they will all flourish through the nurturing of one's own heart.

So, by acknowledging and letting truth reign within you, your life will become even more colourful. And, like a photograph, it can remain as a permanent reminder of your efforts, captured within the lens of light and truth of my heart.

Again, as stated before, by offering neighbours your hand of friendship, the vibrancy and energy can expand between home and home, village and town, city to nation, and to all continents of the world. This will build a new Eden and paradise of love. Effort, determination, trust, and faith will play their part in this, but love is the key to unlocking an easier road towards bliss and peace.

I once mentioned that each life and day given to you is my gift, a present that I have pre-sent, and all you need to do is to determine how to use it. Well, each moment can be a cause for pleasure or pain, of loving memories or disdain, hopes fulfilled, dreams elevated, or emotions evaporated or forgotten—disappearing, as if being sucked down by sewers or drains.

Appreciate then, any waste of your time is a waste of 'life'. Therefore, you only need to decide what to do with it. Can you—or would you—serve others, or should one be self-serving? These are all your own choices. No one can persuade, cajole, or should ever force their will upon another.

These words today may seem more direct and pose more questions than ever before. Timing is everything. One only sees, reads, and hears the 'what, when, and why', precisely at the right moment in every day of their life.

And so, your life does indeed become like the pages of your own diary. Know the past only contains those days that you can reflect upon, unable to change. Once they have been written, those choices and decisions become like huge immovable mountains, which forever attempt to darken one's present thoughts and feelings. Or, perhaps they will glisten and shine like stars and moonlight, evoking memories of happier times and events which can inspire and strengthen your heart, and others, too.

Your future may seem unknown, but this very day both sustains and also creates it. Each second and hour of life provides you with the opportunity to move steadily forward into the reality of your own glory and divine essence. Or one can remain frozen, resembling a broken watch or clock.

As you are part of me, know that I will never leave you. I will always encourage, help, and assist you forever. Therefore, I re-charge you right now —with these words—to balance your positive and negative energy as one, not poles apart. I rewind—and remind—you, so that once again you can move forward with due diligence and fortitude. With hope and faith through your own endeavours, new memories can remain etched within your heart's centre forever These will not fade or disappear by someone else's actions ... or even those so-called hands of time.

Do not fear so-called fate, or even what you feel, or think may become lost, stolen, or taken away from your life. That is only attachment, which leads to anxiety, a lack of contentment, and distrust. No, instead move forward to share the true you. May future days of your life's journey and diary become the permanent record and legacy of your love; whereby your character and personality glow from each page, helping other souls who cross your path, or who join you on the journey of truth.

As you do, love, compassion, and forgiveness will grow for your fellow man and all beings. Division, separation, and any illusion and confusion will become traits of the past. The world—so full of beauty—can once again flourish without the notion of what is yours, or mine. Instead, life will be shared wantonly and willingly, containing the only desire of how this new day can become even brighter, illuminating love and light from all hearts and souls.

And so, do not worry or leave these words behind, resting upon these pages, as I wish you to know of the difference you can make. Understand that you do not differ from 'me'. So, once you have recognized this; any limits imposed ... can only be set by yourself.

I urge you to begin and make your dreams come true. You can achieve so many wonderful and great things in your life. Just believe it and trust in yourself, which leads to the same trust in me.

Write the next page of your diary and life, not only with honesty, but with vigour, passion, and truth. You may actually surprise yourself, but you will never surprise me. Just imagine and create it, for deep inside ... you and I know that you can. Amen.

LESSON 5:

REMORSE

Welcome, as always! On frequent occasions, you just know when to listen, sense, and feel me in your heart. For so many of you, these instances could even arrive after making a so-called 'mistake'. Perhaps this is due to what you think and believe was a wrong decision, causing you to regret your thoughts, words, or deeds.

This will become clearer—and feel much stronger—when it has affected another person, soul, being, animal, or (in fact) any living thing. Can you say how you're actually feeling or thinking at this moment. Maybe something has even occurred today which makes you ache inside? And if so, do your emotions occur this way because of any guilt or remorse?

Please tell me. Yes, please talk to me just like you have done before. But even though I ask you these things right now—in truth—I already know what your heart conveys. This is the same throughout creation as 'I AM I'. Therefore, I understand and comprehend every finite detail, whether it's past, present, or of the so-called future. Ok, so let's begin. You can pretend, or even imagine, I am someone who sits opposite you right now. What is it you wish to say?

"Dear Lord of mercy, I feel I have broken my promise to you. One which I had made so very long ago."

Remind me, my son.

"It was not to hurt any element of life … because we are all one. And that by doing so, don't I just hurt myself?"

Yes, we are 'one', but know this: it is the purpose, the motive and always the intention behind the action which differs between so many hearts of this world today. Likewise, so is the attachment of all of one's surroundings. Be it the car, which is driven, your possessions, and even those of the garden and inner boundary of what you all call 'home' where you each currently live.

Realise that within the well of your heart, tears will only fall if emotions are genuine. These cannot be manufactured or falsely produced. Understand, too, that real tears also glisten and sparkle, whether shed in sadness or joy. Besides, no such 'crocodile' tears can ever deceive me or your own true self.

I know of what you have done today—which makes you feel so sad—but remember the words of a song, once heard many years ago … 'I love you, I'll kill you, but I will love you forever.' Comprehend this once more. Everything of the body is born and so too, that which is grown from a seed, must also die. It is only a question of when.

Remember, everything is light. This is what many calls 'spirit'. So, life must transcend the innate fear of death, which is still so prevalent around the world. As such, the energy of any life form changes through the cycles of life, just as those seasons which bring you winter frosts, spring rain, summer sun, and autumn winds.

Essentially, you all adapt and cope with each. Likewise, when the physical body is cast away from the veil of death, the divine essence of any being and element of creation adjusts—some immediately—while others, because of uncertainty or trepidation, take a little longer for realization to set in.

However, the manner in which 'life' is elevated from the lower vibration of embodiment differs greatly, of course. Most times, pain has gripped the mortal coil for long periods of time-or perhaps even only momentarily—but elements of light and energy feel it. This I cannot deny.

So why would anyone wish to cause such pain upon another? Well, factors which play a part could be karmic, maybe selfishness, or various emotional traits, which even come down to base instincts and/or one's survival.

Appreciate though; does a bird grieve when it pulls a worm up from the ground, to feed its young chicks? Would a fox or owl think twice about catching their prey? Or is the greater need for food and sustenance more powerful, persuasive, and prevalent?

One could deviate and state intelligence, consciousness, and also having a conscience comes into the equation, as each and all have parts to play in the greater and grander scheme of things. Do not misjudge what I say, though. Only human beings can be 'God- aware'. At the same time, this does not mean that animals, creatures, Mother Earth, or any being is—or are—less worthy of my love, or that they cannot feel pain and joy either.

Also, like I have always said, please love the things you think … cannot think. However, there are still countless souls who believe that animals and creatures have little or no intelligence, judging by their small and even microscopic brains, assume they cannot evaluate or understand.

These traits and beliefs are slowly changing by studying communication of life within and upon Mother Nature. Examples of these are between horses, dogs, and man, and even more so with apes and monkeys who can show their feelings and emotions through symbols, pictures, and text. One day, all beings will realise that life involving animals and man is linked far more closely than is currently thought, or ever believed, it could be.

This brings us back to the reasons for this lesson. Does man continue to hack, burn, and cut down, remove, destroy, harm, and kill what is essentially only a reflection of itself? I do not mean in shape, size, or appearance, but in the divine essence which lies inherently within all life and beings. When you can see yourself in another person, animal, tree, flower, creature, and all elements around you, then you have finally grasped that I am everywhere and within everything.

Therefore, 'the God in me is' ... so the initial thoughts of why anyone would wish to harm me, or their self, pose both a question and the answer. In all your decisions, you only need to conclude if something is right or just, and more so, whether it is in the name of love and truth.

Sometimes you may feel you have no choice and that circumstances have dictated that you do 'this, that or the other', but know you only need to trust in yourself, and you'll be trusting in me. Light will always guide you to the right answer. You just need to feel it within you. Appreciate that the gut feeling, your intuition, or the thoughts that enter your mind—which is your conscience—are only from 'I', giving you a gentle nudge to help you in truth.

Always remember, I am within you to help you. So never feel I am even temporarily away, perhaps taking care of what you think are more important issues elsewhere. This can never be the case. I keep reiterating, all creation is me, and all life is whole.

People, creatures, and all beings may seem in pain at certain points in their lives and existence, but recognize that apart from your souls, all traits —and these circumstances—are temporary.

By having strength, fortitude, and perseverance with trust and faith, you can overcome fear and trepidation. By trying to live and conduct oneself in truth, the realization and permanence of love will keep you on the right track. As such, remorse or guilt can never attempt to hold you away from me. Amen.

LESSON 6:
SURROUNDINGS

As always, I welcome you to the connection of our hearts as one. May peace now descend upon all those who bear witness, sense, or feel this upon the planes and dimensions of time and energy and space. Please understand, it is in every soul's nature to desire it above all things. Within peace, the tranquillity and bliss of love sustains all elements of life.

I constantly hear, "Dear Lord (or God), I want peace". So, let me remind you all ... that by eradicating the ego—which is the 'I'—and removing the false desire of the senses (which is your 'want'), you cannot fail to find, or receive, and be left with the peace that is both required and needed.

Some will still ask, "But where is it?" Or "How can I find this peace?" Well, many people will feel influenced by their surroundings. This often leads to thoughts of where they are born—or now live—which could somehow affect such things. Indeed, perhaps one would find it easier to sense and become peaceful if you could hear birdsong, feel sunshine upon your skin, or see fields of green pastures ... maybe a beautiful shoreline, large hills or valleys and mountains?

You may not be in this position, even preferring to be surrounded by the hustle and bustle of a town or city ... those concrete jungles where brick and stone rise and tower overhead. Of course, some hearts 'like' this feeling, for they somehow seem protected within the shadows cast by the sun. Others not at all, for they can feel disconnected from nature and even from life itself. Everyone has opinions of what seems right or wrong in this respect.

Obviously, by living in built-up areas, those who wish to gaze upon the stars at night cannot see them. The glow and illumination from manmade light—emitted from streetlamps, office tower blocks, factories and many other buildings—will cause a halo of haze which blocks out natural beauty from above, and all around you.

Now then, it is important that you understand I am not stating anyone should suddenly vacate, up sticks, and camp out in the hills, because these comparisons are not—in truth—what this lesson is about. The reason I state these things is to explain that you each make the choice of where, what, why, and how you live your life. Even more than this, that you can make your way to the one place where you can comprehend, experience, grow, and know immense beauty and wonderful things by going nowhere!

In fact, there is no material outlay, and no need to cross a palm with notes or coins from any land upon the Earth. Many will comprehend this, already realising I am referring to the connection within their own heart. This place —through the doorway of love—does not need a key. Nor do you need a special password, or any offering to enter. It makes no difference where you physically live or now find yourself at this time.

It is here and here alone within the stillness that noise and distractions of your surroundings, be it any concern, stress, anxiety, fear, or even the walls and barriers which pretend to segregate you from me, will disappear. Time, space, and all the fabric and materials known and unknown to humanity cannot ever divide or separate us, for we are one and whole.

In such times, comprehend, too, that you are already free. You truly are. Those dividing lines erected through different languages and colours of skin are false. They are formed by the illusion and confusion, cast out by those who believe they can manipulate both body and soul ... when they can't.

Remember, throughout history, bodies of many enlightened hearts may have been broken, but the divine essence and spark of love is immeasurable, unique, and eternal. It cannot be cut down by sword or tongue. Nor can it be burnt, buried, or dissolved; it is the only thing which is permanent and everlasting.

So, how do you feel about these words? Do you believe them? If not, could you? Appreciate that you must follow your own truth within yourself. This will lead you to gain wisdom through knowledge and your own life experiences.

This way, every book of text, each person, sage, guru, aspirant, and devotee of truth, can only be deemed as guides. Indeed, they may appear to influence your choices and decisions, but ultimately, it is you and you alone who must decide what resonates inside. You will know what feels comfortable, like your favourite pair of well-worn shoes, which are a perfect fit and seem so right, just as I have often described before.

Take or heed whatever connects with you from this lesson. Perhaps discarding the rest until another page—or day—flows freely inside your heart once more. There is a time for everything. I waste nothing. Therefore, situations and circumstances often repeat themselves in and around you, not to annoy or make one feel upset or desperate, but to show you the way forward. This strengthens you to cope with life's perceived challenges and tests.

For those of later years—especially the retired who have many 'life' experiences—they should be respected. They possess knowledge and wisdom gained through (and from) their periods of work, rest, and play ...

as well as their joy, grief, love, hate, and any fear. Understanding and peace can then be shared, bringing transition, and understanding to the many.

The state often neglects the elderly. Even family or friends may consider them as a burden, but they can become—and should be—revered by every nation. Please comprehend the old and wise, for they are all part of your own 'being', which in turn forms an integral part of society. Therefore, youth and old age should never be deemed as separate, or divided by spans of time, as everyone has their part to play.

Okay then, where do you go from here? Well, you could think about who, what, and why you are who you are. For all that's said and done, there is a role to play and one for you to fulfil. Also, please try not to merge into the background of your 'surroundings'. In doing so, you are like a chameleon—which changes colour through anguish or fear—actually disguising yourself, trying to remain anonymous amongst your kith and kin.

Know too that I do not chastise you. Nor do I expect anyone to desire material accolades, medals, and awards, but urge and wish for you to strive for the greatest prize of all, self-realization into bliss and peace. Through kindness, right conduct, truth, and love, your divine essence, and spark of true creation within, can once more shine like a beacon. You can become a standard bearer and torch carried aloft, like an Olympic flame, which announces the arrival and coming together of all people as one.

This is not a competition between you all, to see who comes 'first'. By the union of souls, each one of you will stay on the right track together. Appreciate that the events of your lives can then become the fields of dreams, encouraging carrying you forward into eternity.

By setting aside the differences in where each of you live, comprehension of the 'one community' prevails. Indeed, as countless people are going through pain and upheaval—from the immense changes within nations and across continents far away from your own—they may still, one day, touch your own shoreline. If not physically … then mentally and emotionally.

The surroundings where you live may currently appear vastly different. That said, the connection of both joy and suffering knows no distance or time to the heart. So, you can never feel alone or isolated from me, even if one somehow denies or hides away from your fellow man.

No … you may all be a living, burning flame of light, but every single one of you are the plumes of my heart. Together, we are whole. So, whether you're living in a mansion, a slum, even a tent or a palace, these material surroundings are impermanent and transitional. Only when you realise that you're forever surrounded by my love and grace will the permanence of truth be retained … eternally resting within your heart. Amen.

LESSON 7:

THE MEADOW

As you think about our 'oneness' and true connection, I ask you to contemplate once more upon the truth from within. At this moment, I implore you to forget—temporarily if you wish—those concerns, needs, or anxieties of the day. Instead of these, I would like you to take a walk with me, together in your mind ... but more importantly, with and through and from the heart.

Please believe then ... that you are now sitting on a garden bench. You are more alert and aware than ever before, remembering and re-learning peacefulness once more. It is a glorious and beautiful sunny morning, and the blue-sky envelops you with clarity of thought. There are no clouds of illusion to cast shadows over the forthcoming journey.

The rays of sun now rise above the valleys and hills in front of you. And as you feel the warmth, a golden path suddenly glistens and glows ... shimmering like a heat haze across the ground, stopping at your feet. This is because you know the reality which lies inside. You fully understand I am no theatrical wizard ... and that this is no make-believe yellow brick road.

You stand up and take your first step upon it, like an innocent child, without caution. Your fear has disappeared. Why should one even fear when you understand I am nearer than near?

You imagine you are walking, but your feet seem to glide along. When you embark upon this journey of truth, it becomes effortless. Know this is because of your energy and resonance, which now elevates you above denser, lower vibrations that try to impose and contain your heart through both the mind and one's senses.

Now, being further and further away from where you started, the gold turns to brilliant white, so intense and all pervading. Strangely, though, you can truly 'see', as your vision of heart, mind, and soul is one. As such, you can bear witness to the splendour and magnificence of me, with new insights into who, what, and why you are 'love'.

Stopping suddenly upon the brow of a hill, you look below to see a meadow of such beauty. Words simply struggle to convey its divine essence and glory. You become eager to visit this paradise of peace and tranquillity. And, because its colours are so vivid, they captivate your heart, transfix your thoughts, and reignite the goal and purpose of the very love inside you.

No shoes are needed here, as your bare feet cross the emerald grass that's softer than silk. Then, as you inhale my breath of life, those lungs are filled with such clean and fresh air; it intoxicates you with its purity.

With 'light' headiness and deciding to sit down, you now pause and reflect for a while within this stillness. The flowers beside you all weave and dance, as if to the merry tune of my heartbeat. Reds, yellows, purples, and blues … in fact, more culminations of every colour imaginable both shine and reflect everywhere. Some appear to grow differently, almost crystallized in appearance, but know these are simply the tears of joy which grow and flourish within my kingdom—shed from both eyes and hearts through love.

These are so precious and cannot be removed or valued as possessions upon the impermanent planes of creation. No, these illuminate and shine eternally through time, space, and dimension; their energy radiating like galactic spirals of fulfilled hopes and wishes into infinity and beyond.

So, they bloom not from fertile soil, but from connections between one heart and another. Perhaps a precious first kiss, the birth of a child, cradling a beloved animal, or by embracing a family member or friend. All are perpetually—and continually—creating the field of dreams.

You close your eyes, then pause and listen to the faint trickle of running water close by. You stand up. Over to the right, its sound becomes magnified. A serene feeling now washes over you. Walking towards the soothing ripples, your hands carefully guide those precious moments of 'joy'—from many hearts—to one side.

Now you're in front of a gentle stream. Its water is so clear that you're amazed to witness the small rainbow coloured fish, swimming effortlessly along the currents of both water and time. Their own destination is to reach the 'source' of love and light in my heart too … knowing, believing, and instinctively continuing the journey 'home'.

New feelings suddenly cascade over you, arriving by glorious birdsong from the nearby trees and bushes. There, sitting upon a branch—which hangs suspended by my love over the water—is a Kingfisher; so elegant, beautiful, and colourful you become frozen by its majestic brilliance.

Its colours glow within an aura of gold and white, symbolic of the 'Son'. He waits for the attention of unsure hearts and minds … happy to shine and lead you as a King; a fisher of men, women, and all of humankind. But only the soul and heart can decide whether to follow. For always and forever, each one will make their own decision in this lifetime, or maybe ... the next.

Though captivated and enthralled by these sights and sounds, therein lies the need to continue onwards. Perhaps you'll move forward over a small bridge, to cut across troubled waters of your own current of emotions? Or, instead, by taking the steppingstones which lay down before you—to ease both past and present burdens. This route requires more effort on your part, for each one is a leap of faith, enabling you not only to trust yourself but also me. If you have the belief, then you'll understand untold strength and power are inherent within you.

Karmic imbalance will turn to 'right action', which will bring new focus, purpose and meaning into your life. Thereby, in truth, with perseverance and fortitude, it will bloom with the sweet fragrance and perfume of love, to be shared to and through, and from all whom you meet. Either way, these pastures new have beckoned. They have called you, pulled upon heart strings to meet the challenge of one's embodiment. Not just for now but guiding and leading you for all eternity.

Suddenly, high above you, in the light blue backdrop, a lone golden eagle appears almost motionless, somehow able to float upon and in the ether. Know that it is I, surveying and watching over your decisions, motives, action, thoughts, and words.

I am no spy in the sky, but forever seek to guide, protect, and promise that I will swoop and defend you against the predators of both inner and outer demons. Understand that together, it is easier to crush the ego and any selfish traits, and be able to treat criticism and praise, elation and condemnation with impartiality and equanimity. Remember; do not fear, for I am near.

Now realising that the sun is about to set, you look around for the continuing path of light, as if to return from where you feel you came. Consider this though, that you are already 'home', and you will always return to self. Try to understand too, that the feeling of warmth which seems to disappear over the horizon is but a mirage, because love and light are forever constant, not dictated by distance or by any such earthly time zones.

So, whether it appears night or day, if something feels that it is so-called 'good or bad', or even right or wrong, always live by your own truth inside your heart. Remember, in all that you think or say or do, if it is with right conduct, peace, and with love, no one can ask any more of you.

In recognition of such, you'll find yourself sitting back once more, on the same garden bench, rested and cradled within the seat of your soul.

Now, as you are there again, you can fully appreciate your heart and love are the jewels upon my crown. It shines eternal, reflecting and attracting you all upon your journeys of self–realization into bliss.

Let me remind you once more, you are each a spark of the divine flame of my heart … not divided or separated, but truly whole. You are, indeed, all of creation itself. If or when you should ever doubt this, you can always return to the peace, tranquillity, and the stillness, and to the meadow of your very core. Amen.

LESSON 8:

NUTS AND BOLTS

Will you find the time today to draw close to us and our connection? I hope so, because I wish to welcome you once more to re-learn and digest the truth. Then you'll understand and get to the crux and the 'nuts and bolts' of the matter at hand. What is this I speak of? And by what means, or route should you take in your forthcoming days, weeks, months, and years?

First, appreciate I could also pre-empt this whole 'lesson' by again asking you how you feel today, as your answer would surely show one's current thoughts, concerns, and feelings to all those around you. They would also reveal whether you are actually trusting in both yourself and in 'I', to guide and provide you with what you presently need at this point in your life.

Therefore, become more aware that 'life' can sometimes seem clouded. Certain situations appear to make no sense at all, at least until a much later date. For example, please consider someone who needs to spend time with a friend or their next of kin who is unwell.

Maybe, through an apparent twist of fate, a unique chain of circumstances—which seems bizarre at first—enables a person to do so. Perhaps it is redundancy, a change of working hours, a financial windfall, a compassionate leave of absence, or even an injury to oneself which removes you from your current situation ... and they are all options which could occur and provide the opportunity you require to both aid and support another person. Understand I will never interfere with your actual choices, for they will always be up to you and you, alone. You must decide what is important—or not—as the case, maybe.

Again, as the title of this lesson suggests, it is all, and it is everything. This leads to the very core and heart of the matter. Remember, when the right scenario has been created, it occurs with honesty and love ... like a nut and bolt which fits perfectly together. However, when someone's feelings, thoughts, and deeds become selfish, then one is misaligned from the truth. It is like the bolt becoming cross threaded; the nut having been forced against its will.

Unconditional love never flows like this. The nut would flow effortlessly around the bolt without friction or complication, as if one doesn't even have to think ... it just happens. Communication between two people—or even two nations—can resemble this too, because when they tolerate and accept their individual ways of life, it draws them closer together. Only by the understanding and knowing of such, is one able to exist in harmony with each other's characters, personalities, and differences.

That said, if distrust, fear, or hatred rise to the surface of hearts or minds, bonds can be broken, ties severed, and the connection no longer flows freely. It is as if it has been neglected or isolated, becoming stuck fast with rusty attitudes, a simple reflection of those old and outdated ways of living and learning.

What is really important to each other—and every one of you—is that things are far more difficult after such a situation has occurred. Appreciate that in trying to free or rather force the nut from the bolt can cause some irreparable harm. Like cutting deep into the very fabric of one's being.

The traces of damage, which are caused to the very threads that keep one together, are easily seen—like an open wound of the flesh. Or they can appear almost invisible, such as a broken heart … deceived and hurt by another's words, thoughts, actions, and deeds.

So, do you see where I am coming from regarding this theme of text? The nut and bolt can only function together. Separately, they become isolated, their purpose undefined, gathering dust in the corners of boxes and draws, or moreover, inside both hearts and minds.

There should be no division. Both depend upon each other, like a brother and sister, a husband and wife, and both you and I; it is together that we are whole. Just as the positive needs a negative, without the darkness, the light could not see or know itself, either. This is the simplicity of this lesson. I require it to be understood deep within your heart.

Please accept there is nothing within 'life' which exists without its purpose to fulfil. Of this, we can talk about things as the warmth and light from the sun, the gravitational pull of the moon, the fragrance of a flower, a song from a bird, the hub of a wheel, and even the foundations of a house … the list would be endless. It matters not whether you consider material or non-material elements of such an equation. They all represent both the cause and effect of life and existence throughout creation.

One may now consider the question regarding your very own life—its purpose and task—but again, this is simply just to be whom and what you are, a divine spark of love and light. Therefore, every day you can illuminate all that's around you, but will you? Would you really expect to turn a light switch on, and the bulb not to shine?

With an open heart and soul and mind, you can truly send out rays of hope and warmth in every thought, word, and deed. These will reflect your own individuality far and wide, and yet at the same time, help to unify and link humanity as 'one'.

Of course, I realise people throughout the world will often think they are different. They cannot—or do not wish to—see eye to eye. In truth, the 'I' in each of you are the same fragment and spark of me ... but just within different bodies. The spoken tongue is the element which enables the very challenges or so-called tests, trials, and tribulations of the people to be worked through and accomplished.

Understand then, every heart needs only to decide what they should do with their time. Remember, also, hands that 'do' are holier than lips that pray. So, by giving something of the real 'you' to another person, to society and humanity, one leaves a trace ... an echo of kindness reverberating across time, space, and many dimensions.

Likewise, comprehend each moment where you serve another as also serving me—and ultimately yourself, too. Whatever is done in truth cannot be a selfish act, unlike someone who is looking to gain something in return.

Remember, you are all given what you need, and not always what you think you want. This way, you can move forward in my trust with the belief and knowledge everything is as it should be. From here, you can reach beyond the stars, because in, through, from, and to 'love'... the sky has no limits, and no bodily limitations imposed upon you either.

Comprehend that it is your true self, which is the greatest discovery of all. You haven't even had to travel or go anywhere else to find this truth! You are the miracle ... the be all and end all. And yet you were, are, and forever will be, from no beginning to meet no end.

Just as light is eternally expanding throughout creation, the same love and energy inside your heart is too. But it will always require, need, and truly desire the truth from within, because it is all sustaining and pervading.

Therein, the thirst for knowledge, experience, and wisdom is always quenched. I will never refuse or ration you, either. The well of your heart is without end, and it is forevermore your aim to accept or deny it. No force or coercion will ever make you feel pressurized into believing someone or something which does not currently resonate deep inside.

Having now read this lesson, only you can decide whether we have gotten to the nuts and bolts, the 'nitty-gritty', and the so-called crux of the matter. Perhaps you can now make time to be 'still'. You may just find the passion and reason for your life within you now. On the other hand, maybe other tasks will take precedent ... but understand this; such choices are your own and will always be up to you to make. Amen.

LESSON 9:
CLARITY

I welcome hearts and souls from every form of life to sense and know the truth. Furthermore, I hope—by the end of these few pages—you will find a clearer view of where you are headed and what's needed and required for you to become fulfilled ... and therefore be at peace within yourself.

So, how will you begin or end your day? Will it be with optimism, enthusiasm, and excitement for the challenges which lie ahead? Or does a feeling of trepidation, uncertainty, or frustration attempt to grip you? Will this prevent you from experiencing the truth of whom, what, why and where you are at this present time?

If the latter is the case, one could easily visualize a dense fog, rolling down the hills and rising in the valleys. It blurs and attempts to hide your true vision of mind and body, and soul. Sometimes, such days may feel as if there is no escape. They seem to overtake, overwhelm, and confuse you.

However, please try to understand that life can take these turns. These are the days where there appear to be too many decisions to make. I bear witness as you look for the answers to your family, work, or home 'situations'. And many people appear to be wondering around, unable to see the wood from the tress, or even their own hands in front of their face.

You must all realise uncertain times for what they are ... temporary and fleeting phases. So, instead of believing that the unknown weakens you, or having negative responses to circumstances with which you assume—often mistakenly—are out of your control, just try to change your mindset.

Only love is permanent. So, whatever is occurring cannot last forever. It does not matter what way you perceive or how you look at it. Hence, like the power of the Sun, which brings light every day to banish darkness, so, too, the mind can refocus to clear these clouds of illusion and confusion. Then, the fog upon those hills and in the valleys will eventually change to mist. It elevates. To your senses, it will seem to have disappeared—from, through, and by rays of heat from above, and also from the love within.

Know it is I then who—through your heart's centre—will empower you to rise above such times, clearing the way with determination and truth to live your life with honesty and integrity. Therefore, please trust and believe your own strength lies inside you. In time, you'll know that what is seen through the eye (I) of the heart can differ greatly from the eyes of your body.

Those true windows—of opportunity—to behave and display the traits of a kind and helpful human being may once have been obscured. Or they seem distant (like blurred far away objects becoming difficult to distinguish), but by removing the impediments of doubt and fear, you will refocus on important decisions and goals, and those many responsibilities in your life.

In fact, every day, your surroundings—and society—will knowingly, or unknowingly, attempt to trick or disguise what is seen, felt, or heard by your senses. If these are not filtered through discretion and morality, or even by one's own faith, such elements enter the mind, becoming displayed once more through desire, anguish, hatred, and fear by what you think and say and do.

It is vital, therefore, to separate the wheat from the chaff. One must pick what feels right for you during work, rest, and play. Sometimes this will be easy, other times not so. For example, imagine for a moment you are listening to relaxing music upon an old cassette tape, which has since become crinkled or twisted … instead of hearing the pure melody or notes, they will only resemble background noise, a distortion in the voice of truth.

So, one needs to iron out, re-tune, and refocus to understand what is being said or portrayed. I can assist and guide you. But I cannot do this for you because your own inner journey—utilising discernment—will need and want to grow through one's own experience to become 'wise'. If I lay all the answers out before you, your own efforts would wish to—and more often than not—take an easier road or route every single time.

Of course, some of you, either for karmic reasons (or to assist other souls), aren't in this position, whereby you constantly have to make difficult choices and decisions on the road ahead. Also, one cannot achieve and attain wisdom through another's eyes or heart. It is the one journey that you must undertake with me, 'together' … for you are not, and never will be, alone.

Therefore, with the aid of these books, but more importantly with my love in your heart—as a guide, teacher, confidant, friend, and companion who is forever within, above, below, and by your side—you can continue with fortitude and determination towards self-realization and bliss … into peace.

Do not idle in your endeavours. Nor become affected by anyone else's influence unless it connects and resonates with your own truth inside. If you feel happiness and contentment—and it brings meaning to you—then all must be well … because negativity, fear, or distrust would make you feel out of sync, apprehensive, and uncertain.

Do not believe this will eternally side-track you; it won't. All truth leads to me. A 'detour' of experience often helps to keep you focused, for it gives prompts and clues about your own inner search and thirst for knowledge. Through discrimination, you can then make the right choices from and through and to the heart.

Comprehend that any limitations are false. They are the subject of the subconscious mind. This only tries to see the future by focusing on the past. It can release negativity through irrational thoughts and subsequently affect your behaviour. That said, it can still protect you. It does this by rationalizing your decisions, stopping you from purposefully harming yourself, unless one is mentally or emotionally impaired through illness, disease, or by various forms of abuse. It is appropriate to always be on your guard. I will help you by being your conscience, which pricks the mind … as well as your intuition, providing those gut feelings swelling over you when something feels right or wrong.

So, if you can trust in me, you will trust in yourself. As we are 'one', you will need no other false declarations of support to help carry you when days seem tough and/or when others despair. You can be the strength for those who cannot see the light and wish to cling to you. You can help encourage, motivate, and lead—as and when required to do so—because you know, and also see, the truth both within and out.

With the understanding that 'life' can be what you make of it—even in desperate times—I am there if you look for me. I am the smile, the birdsong, and the lone flower amongst the weeds of discontentment and hurt and anger. I am the softly spoken words to encourage and help, the comforting arm during tears of grief, and the stranger who assists you in the hour of need. Yes, I am the love, the light, and am all things in all places.

I promise I will wipe away and cleanse the anguish of every heart and soul. You will see, feel, and sense me more clearly than ever before. And because love knows no bounds, it is free from time and distance, all the while permeating and transcending every plane and dimension of energy and vibration.

You are this same power and magnificence. Believe it to be so and nothing, absolutely nothing, can prevent you from making your hopes, dreams, and your eternal goal come true. Finally, today, please appreciate that having clarity of thought is an immense step. It leads to a clearer vision of whom, what, and why you are, and—as mentioned earlier—where you're headed to. Amen.

LESSON 10:
EVERYTHING

I welcome all who draw close to me. May you understand, feel, and know these words written upon a page, which are being etched into the mind and heart and soul. In doing so, realise that so many voices ask or cry out to me, "Dear God, please teach me what I need to know."

Some will even request that I impart everything they require ... to help them achieve their true essence. However, if I was to do this, one's mind and brain would simply explode. The 'body' upon the 'earth-plane' could not cope with such truth—love and light's 'vibration and energy'—in its current form.

So, each one of you grows and knows precisely and exactly what you need and require at any given time. This influences and affects the individual and also, of course, those who are close by, such as your family and friends.

Now, as you sit in the garden upon this new day, the Sun is shining. Its warmth radiates down and through your being. For those who are not currently experiencing the same, perhaps you could try to picture it within your mind's eye instead.

As different sights, sounds, and smells fill your senses, peace reigns supreme. Freshly hung washing on the line tries to compete with the fragrances of Mother Nature, but everything 'manmade' dissipates and fades by the minute, hour, day, and week.

Birdsong elevates the thoughts above the sound of any mode of transport —those fleeting and momentary noises which can disturb the untrained mind. Remember, I am their soft, subtle tones and the calls you can hear across the airwaves of the ether. I am also their cries and shrieks when they face danger from man or nature.

The sky above is clear and blue. This allows the rays of Sun fall, casting shadows both here and there. Likewise, do not fear the same in any areas of your life. Rather, one should embrace them as the times when you can grow and experience any test, trial, or tribulation, which strengthens you to gain wisdom.

Indeed, many periods of life will be lived in the 'grey'. One can never live totally in the light, or stay perpetually in darkness, either. However, one's soul—deep inside—eternally, needs to seek the right path, enabling you to live, learn, grow, and share the love inside your heart.

The shadow or middle ground between the up and down, and the within and out, not only provides and helps the 'doer' but also those whose lives connect with one's own. This way, love flows like blood throughout the veins. It touches and feeds the vital organs of the body. Likewise, the light is connected to all life and all nature, which is the universal 'body' of man and all creation.

One may often feel or think they can become separate from me though, as if a so-called 'accident'—or for medical reasons—has removed a limb. But no, this is unattainable. Unless the person's mind is incapacitated, even by removing a limb, they can still sense the essence of it.

Therefore, division from me is impossible, but after so much has been learnt, you can now distinguish that the body and soul are truly separate. How else can your dreams take you to amazing and beautiful places? How could you experience wonderful joy for both your heart and soul? Indeed, the body rests in sleep, but your soul continues to strive, learn, and share the true and real you.

The body, or so-called 'overcoat', is so important for your earthly work, rest, and play. This sheds like a second skin, but is never discarded until fully worn out or after your karmic imbalance has been fulfilled. This might occur after one second, one minute, one hour, one week, one month, one year or three scores and ten (or more) have been experienced and past.

Know that throughout the years since your birth, all of humankind seeks and strives to accumulate and attach themselves to each other and those earthly impermanent traits and desires. Through work and education, one will wish to gain money, and then increase one's wealth by buying property and vehicles. Through marriage too, children may come along and thus the cycle of new attachments continues for many years.

Until one day, each one of you detaches yourselves, knowingly or unknowingly, through the later years of your life ... but how? Well, retirement brings loss of work and/or income. Old age sees grandparents and parents drift into the permanence of light once more. Your children may leave home, while friends or family may move or fade away, and all the while, connections seem to weaken or disappear to leave you seemingly alone. But you're never alone—and can never be—as I am captivated from, through, and to your heart, remember?

Throughout the eons of time, there are some who know and share this truth. Many call them the ascended masters. They know they're always 'one' and will forever place clues in thoughts, words, and deeds. These souls understand light can never diminish and can eternally be traced through truth. You only need to discover the same—deep inside your heart.

Try to 'unearth' the reality that is inside you, unlike discovering the fossils and relics of life from countless creatures who have lived and roamed millions and billions of years ago. Many so-called secrets of life are a mere thought away, below the surface of ego, hate, anger, and jealousy. You do not need to dig through layers of hardened granite and natural stone to reveal the true meaning of life.

Even to this day, new skeletons are revealed—preserved by peat or bog—and primitive man or dinosaurs will always display a great deal of information for the academics and scientists to dissect. However, all methods acquired so far by humanity—to both evaluate and debate such complex components like DNA—will fail. They cannot interpret the 'why' of creation and its purpose, even though they may understand the where and when.

Life, and more importantly, love, cannot be scanned, cut open, or even exposed this way. Truth does not need a microscope or telescope to make a leap of faith, or enable one to view the glory and divine essence of you and me.

I urge you to understand that the 'everything'—which so many seek—is all around and within you. You are 'creation' in action. You all have an immense power that can only be imagined.

So now, as countless people ask for answers to this, that, and the other—whether that is from the mind or from the heart—please know that you actually know it already! When you seek with and through the truth, then the complexities of your life will fall away. The mind will become eased of both worry and stress, and the heart will not skip a beat through fear or dread.

Likewise, if you can appreciate that the Sun forever shines—even when it's night or day—then so too your light cannot dissipate but may only become hidden through one's own traits or karma. Therefore, I ask you to remove this blanket of confusion and illusion. Please illuminate your own pathway to leave all shadows behind in your wake. This is eternally the truth … and this truth is eternal. Amen.

LESSON 11:
QUEST

You are all most welcome to our connection, to aid and complete the goal and quest of every heart and soul in creation. Before we begin today, please understand that from the moment of one's re-birth to the 'earth-plane', you are all seeking both happiness and love.

It is apparent, from the instant the senses realise your new embodiment—with a lamenting cry—this inherent need and desire can never leave you. Appreciate it is only on a soul level that you will know of the tasks to complete and your karma to clear and balance. There can be no other way.

So, love is usually bestowed upon a baby by its doting parents … who become mesmerized by the precious gift which lies before them. There is no separation or division. Even though a new life is detached from the mother, it would normally become attached emotionally—and internally—by those eternal heart strings.

Then, as the body grows, so does the brain. Through the system of education, one hopefully learns skills and the means to survive and live upon the earth … and within the society of humanity. During these early years, it is important to understand that you are here for a reason, other than to accumulate additional baggage—which one can do without—whether it is physical, mental, or emotional.

One may say this is easier said than done. Of course, it is. Only through experience can you gain wisdom. No one can cheat or assume—by some sort of extra revision—that it will somehow enable them to speed through the process, or even pretend it is of no concern.

As such, why are you here? Has some bizarre set of circumstances made you who you are today, or placed you in your exact position of work, family, health, or wealth? One may assume that it is you who is always the 'doer', but this is not necessarily so. Appreciate it is I who knows what, when, and why you need what you need, and to receive everything through your own, or by another's hand. However, do not misinterpret what I mean or say here. Ultimately, it is still your own search, goal, and quest for the truth, which enables you to re-learn this purpose of your life.

Therefore, during your 'worldly' years, I request you do not ask me how important you are in the grand scheme of things … because as I have said before, each grain of sand upon every desert and beach is vital, for it makes one whole.

No doubt, there will be long periods where soul searching and the craving for answers will ring like the chimes of a bell into eternity. "Why me? What must I do? What shall I become? Is this all there is? I want to be happy. Where is the love?" The list seems endless because the mind thinks too much, threatened by its own demise and self-importance—once the heart has become the focal point of truth.

As the heart's centre is soft, precious, and all giving, it doesn't like to upset the mind. It tries to appease it with rationalization, when in fact this can weaken resolve, thus causing you to become confused and indecisive. All this leads to never ending circles of illusion and those 'push me–pull you' or those 'should I or shouldn't I' scenarios. But direct action and determination need to be the primary focus and aim for the soul instead.

These oscillating periods can bring sadness, discontentment, and strain between connections of family and friends. Each of your lives seems headed in different directions ... when, ideally, your lives should become intertwined to support and help each other.

Indeed, I see these fractured emotions and many red eyes (I's) from tears having fallen, which then leave traces and scars across hearts resembling ploughed fields. However, in your weakness, if you trust in both me and you, I will make you strong once again. New seeds of opportunity and growth will find their way up—and through—the fertilized soil (soul), being blessed by my grace, grown with my love, and sustained by my light.

By cultivating and finding one's own truth, and following it with passion and integrity, your hopes and dreams will rise and flourish. You just need to believe it. That said, as your life then progresses, you may still succumb to negative feelings and look back upon these phases and think, 'Where did it all go wrong?' Or 'How and why was I so happy back then?' Well think! What were you doing at that time compared to now? How were you feeling? Who or what has or is currently influencing you?

Please, try not to blame anyone else for how you think or feel, as all souls are a reflection of each other. You must realise it is you who is responsible for every decision you make for yourself. Only you can control how you feel and deal with your emotions. It is vital too that guilt is not passed to another via one's own traits of personality, character, or demeanour, with the desire to control or influence someone or something else. Remember, I am the Indweller of all hearts. When you inflict pain in any form upon another, then not only is that pain directed at me, but it can also reflect on yourself.

So, now we have come full circle ... from, through and to your 'self', with the quest and goal—being self-realization—which leads to eternal bliss and peace. Know then that as the Sun rises each day, it brings a new dawn for all souls. For some, the quest will simply mean getting through their day of challenges and perceived problems. For others, this may just be trying to survive—from a lack of food or water—so 'peace' may appear furthest from their minds.

For many more, it will bring overwhelming joy, feeling love from, to, and through them in a multitude of expressions. Perhaps it is a kiss with your husband, wife, or partner. Maybe it is in seeing the glory of creation in the Sun, the Moon, or the stars. What about feeling raindrops upon your skin, the wind in your hair, or hugging a member of your family or a friend … it might even be your beloved pet by your side.

Indeed, love resonates in truth, and truth resonates in love. Any being or beast cannot confine it. Time or distance cannot divide or separate light and darkness, nor can they ever erase it.

Man may continue to travel and quest through space and eventually cross galaxies, but the inner quest of all souls bears greater relevance and importance. This is not a 'mission impossible' but can be achieved by the desire and determination of every heart and soul.

Please comprehend too, my guiding hand does not elevate above any self-destruct button. It is for each one of you to decide what to do with the time that you have been given. Deem each moment as a gift, a present which I have 'pre-sent' to you, as I have continually stated.

So, do what you will and 'will' what you do, knowing that your thoughts will act like keys, unlocking those doors of opportunity you had imagined were locked. Enter and explore every avenue your new path reveals to you. Your life, your destiny and very existence wish to thrive and glow anew. Believe, trust, and have faith in yourself … and keep shining, like you and I know that you can. Amen.

LESSON 12:

PATHWAYS

I welcome all those who have seemingly 'travelled' from near or far—overcoming trepidation and fear—to become a witness to my love. So, do you feel that you have overcome some great distance? Or have you (in truth) drawn closer to me in no time at all … as in the blink of an eye ('I')?

Please comprehend that there are so many roads and pathways in all of creation. Therefore, it is often called the 'pathless' path. Each provides a 'choice less' choice, or moreover, a chance to become whom I really meant you to be. Understand, though, that throughout your current embodiment, it is so natural to look and take the so-called easier route. It is an attempt to evade all of life's pitfalls, in the belief it can somehow bring you more quickly—or closer—to me.

Others, meanwhile, accept the way forward with challenges being met head on. So, when you embark upon the voyage of discovery called life—with both integrity and honesty—then truth not only becomes your guide but is also your protection. Like an umbrella, it will cast aside the fall of emotions which flow incessantly from the mind, trying to influence and direct your heart.

In contrast, your sojourn—you could read this as 'soul-journey'—really has only one route or path to undertake. It is the inner path and is your very own. Hence, no written word, guru, or saint, can walk it for you. Neither would you wish them to. As a result, if you see—or ever feel—that there's a secret or divine explanation, or indeed any other magical formulae which explains that you can have access to reality by any other means other than through thy heart, then they are surely mistaken.

That said, only you yourself can make that judgment call. Simply accept what resonates within you and what doesn't. Remember, I will never be your judge and jury. You are each forever your own.

So, where do you believe you are right now? Do you sense or feel mystified by circumstances around you at this present time? Are you uncertain of your thoughts and actions? Have you stopped trusting in yourself and in me? Indeed, it can be natural for many of you across the 'earth-plane' to feel uncertain right now, in times of economic and global turmoil, though perhaps it would be unnatural to feel anything else. Or would it?

As this is an important period upon the Earth's calendar, millions of people (over Easter) will wish to refocus—perhaps even re-align—their thoughts and hearts … remembering Lord Jesus upon the cross and his resurrection.

But no matter what religion you follow, one's faith can be strengthened, or even renewed at any time, but especially more so now. How much emphasis it bears in your life is also down to the individual and your own feelings and emotions flowing through your being. This will help you feel more—or possibly less—connected to me and to love, which is the source and energy of all things.

Appreciate that love is uncomplicated, being simple in its manifestation of, from, and throughout all creation. This is the one path that—if followed —will never lead you astray, or into disarray. It is the beacon of truth … an eternal flame, just like the spark of divinity within your own heart's centre.

It does not need any man-made or impermanent method to light the way ahead. No 'streetlamps' are required to see where you are going. Your own pathway is already illuminated if you can trust all is as it should be.

Do you ever feel or think that I do not know what you need or want? Are you currently assuming that decisions you make are entirely your own? Can you hear me as your conscience, or those gut feelings or intuition? And are you actually relying upon your mind alone to discover what it thinks are the safest and most desirable routes to take you forward, based on your own experiences or those of others around you?

Mmm … people will often state that if you do not have a plan, then you are planning to fail. But in whose eyes, and by what standard or expectation, is this? One must realise that it is your own responsibility to understand all paths lead to me, so how can you fail? You only need to decide—and finally comprehend—that not only are you more than a 'body,' but you are precious beyond compare.

Understand too, all the accolades and so-called success given by one person upon another, or even by society, are all by-products of life. They come to fruition, though all will become residues of the past. Unlike love, which is forever glorified and polished by my grace. Therefore, by striving and in living to be the best human being you can be, with truth, non-violence, right conduct, peace—and with love—all the exterior trappings of earthly success, whether this is fame or fortune, one's health or friendships, can all individually (or collectively) cross the road that you take.

In contrast, when one walks or travels along negative routes, beholding traits of hate, jealousy, anger, pride, and ego, then one's life, whether past, present, or future—if so required—will reflect this. Every soul and their karmic burden must be dissolved and eradicated, placed into the fire of truth, so that the living flame can turn the imbalance into ash.

It is self-perpetuating. Goodwill brings goodwill—and God's will—and though ill-favoured deeds may seem to be hidden or forgotten, I remember them upon your own scales of justice and truth. Everything is balanced. Effect always follows cause, no matter whom, what, where, or why in all of existence. Consequently, do not deem yourself too small or too big, somehow thinking that one is above or below such things, as the eyes of truth are forever watching over you.

Do not think that you can keep a secret from your true 'self' either … or from me. Likewise, do not feel that one deserves more—or less—than you think you (or they) ever should. When you fully understand and know that I love you beyond comprehension, self-realization becomes the reality. This will lead you to every aspect of your life.

So, by comprehending that you are I and I am you, the weight, and burdens that you have brought with you—and may have collected—upon your current pathway, will fall away (or so you may think), for it is I who will carry them instead, with my blessing and 'All That I Am'. I do not separate you from me. I will only ever let you carry what you can bear at any one time. This is my promise.

Some days you will feel you are trying to drag a dead weight behind you, with the struggle immense, and the pressure of responsibility or desire almost unbearable. As there are so many types of pain, be it physical, mental, or emotional, some will feel worse than others. But you only need to think of me and feel me in your heart to know that I am right there with, besides, above, below, within, and out of you. Therefore, how can you ever be alone?

You are my friend, brother, sister, husband, wife, partner, King or Queen … and everything beyond and in between. You can, from this day forth, resurrect your flame of faith, hope, and charity. For together—as one—we can not only illuminate your own pathway ahead, but enable any aspect of life that may have fallen by the wayside, to sense and see the aspect of true life and love. This eternally shines from your heart through my own. In doing so, you thereby assist and guide them towards finding their own pathway too. Amen.

LESSON 13:
OCEANS

Welcome once more to every soul who links and joins this voyage of self-discovery and love. Therefore, it is so poignant—is it not—that so many of you are currently thinking about the earth's oceans, which cover most of the world and habitat. And now, almost 100 years to the day has passed since the Titanic plunged towards the murky depths below. Submerged it may be —but never forgotten in either minds or hearts.

Indeed, much has been said or debated about fate or destiny. Whether the passengers and crew on board had ever lost faith and hope, and of who had been brave, and who—perhaps—were not. Please know I always hear those who fear. All cries resemble echoes, rebounding from every vessel, from both man-made impermanent ships and those of the body which house every soul.

Please realise that your physical being—almost entirely made of water—can float, bob, and weave and rise and fall upon the sea of emotions. In reality, you may travel by all modes of transport, but when stripped bare to your divine essence, you simply merge as one wave upon the sea of love. Therefore, I ask you not to be afraid of 'death'. And know that there were many on board who did not … each performing their duty to the last, placing the well-being of others even before their own safety.

Within those icy depths and the darkness of the night, the music played, and the call and transmission for help (c.q.d/s.o.s.) continued to reverberate like an irregular heartbeat. Understand too, it was not 'I' who would ever place any man, woman or child into a so-called class or category. One's illumination and effluence are not confined to age, sex or education, the clothes you wear, or even the colour of your skin, hair or eyes.

No. It is for you and your own mind to decree that earthbound conditions and circumstances lead to such events, and not 'fate'. Or that many souls' own choices and desires can initiate the unthinkable or sink the 'unsinkable'.

Comprehend then, as you each embark upon the never-ending tide of emotions, you may succumb to both positive and negative thoughts. And of these, try to realise which ones will eventually guide you or tie you down, like clinging to driftwood floating upon the current, to those unknown shores of anguish and anxiety.

By believing in yourself, you will also appreciate I am your mast and the sails to carry you along to where you truly belong. So you are not lost. Not to me. And, if you somehow feel doubtful of my love, or become disorientated by a whirlpool of desire through the impermanent world, reach for our connection within your heart, and I will instantly bring you to safer, calmer waters.

Any turbulence which seems to overshadow your decision making can, if left unchecked, keep you unfocused. It will even try to deny the truth of whom and what you are. Try then—for a moment—to imagine a ship without a rudder, or a boat with no oars. How could you steer? Well, in fact, you do not even need to try! But how—or why—can this be? Know that your faith and your trust can replace them, and even below the surface, with the undercurrent of what can seem troubled times, there is the strength within your heart to guide you upon the right course and action.

As I have said before, your destiny will be to reach the shore of truth. So, by removing the anchor (anger) of confusion and illusion (which weighs you down), you will soon comprehend self-realization will lead you towards your goal. No longer will you try to sail upon the ocean of doubt, which has always attempted to keep you from knowing your true 'self' and me.

Within and out, I am nearer than near. Therefore, do not visualize the shore as being too distant or separate from you. Just like two sides of a coin, the land and sea are both opposites, and yet one contains the other. They are inseparable and depend upon each other to reveal their true beauty and reality, as do you and I.

Indeed, you are both my expression and my 'body', whilst I am the eternal flame within your heart that can never part. As such, what do you wish to do? Where do you now want to be? Are you trying to overcome or navigate around some seemingly impossible obstacle? Is there an iceberg of mountainous proportions blocking your view towards the new horizon for your soul? And how are you feeling right now? What is your mind, and more importantly your heart, trying to tell you?

More often than not, if you can try to accept all life with the so-called good and bad times with equanimity, then whatever obstruction is in your path will dissipate. Even the iceberg which contains the memory—and layers—of countless winters eventually fades. The problem is never too big … because no matter the size, it will eventually melt and merge into the emotional waters of your existence.

By trying not to force whatever issue surrounds you, then the love and light within can shine on it. This will dissolve your 'problem' or concern. It will always help if your expectation of immediate results is dampened down as, more often than not, to achieve different tasks and fulfil hopes and dreams takes time and much effort. Thus, it is down to the individual if they wish to persevere, maintaining a desire to reach their own personal goal.

Understand, too, that the ocean bed is littered with many vessels who either knowingly—or unknowingly—failed to reach their destination. There are those who took a greater risk with other peoples' lives beside their own, and those who made duty and honour an eternal sacrifice. And then, there are people who made foolish actions, all the while emitting cries which now resonate and echo throughout waves of time and emotion.

By this, one may believe that I state or assign some sort of blame. As always, I am not any soul's judge or jury. I do not strike down or lift any 'body' upon a whim, even though, of course, I could. So then, does this mean I neglect you, or that I am a distant source that one can seldom reach? Of course not!

Let me explain further. As you appreciate you can never be alone, then there can be no separation or division. As this is so, how can a spark of divinity lose their way, make incorrect choices that obscure the truth from yourself and each other? Well, know that over many incarnations and embodiments, each soul wishing to express 'love' has done these things, and has therefore become imbalanced. Hence, many millennia have passed, but still uncertainty has flourished while hurt, pain, and anguish reached new heights.

With this said, many will assume I am harsh. And, as I am omnipotent and omnipresent that I can—or should—surely repair all such ills. Once again, I could, but one must remember, as you are me and I am you ... you have the same power within. How could you not have? So, through your own spiritual development and illumination, you can achieve and restore balance to every aspect of your being yourself!

In order to do so, you must cleanse all the sticky black molasses which has accumulated around your heart and the divine flame within. To help you, try to imagine what these may look like. Think about an oil spill which oozes from a damaged hull of a ship, or from an oil rig disaster. It is unrefined and raw, just like the negativity and imbalance just mentioned. Indeed, it clings like a dark shadow, for oil and water do not mix. It can therefore take a lot of effort to cleanse it from the sea of tranquillity in which your heart resides.

Like a bird, fish, or any form of life tainted by it, just thrashing about will not loosen its vice like grip. However, by clarity and cleanliness of thought, word, and deed, you can begin to eradicate and remove the toxins of inherent karma. Once started, the process can only get easier. Then, like the bird which can now fly, and the fish that can swim once more in purer, cleaner waters, you can realise the same freedom you already have.

I AM I The Indweller of Your Heart—Book Three

So, wipe away all darkness and fear. You can disembark from the pretend leisure cruise of the impermanent world, to seek the true horizon beyond both visions and dreams. Then, as the water becomes calm—just like a millpond—you will gaze upon your own reflection, and see the sun (Son) aglow, radiant, and everlasting ... and the true you. Amen.

LESSON 14:
PURITY

May this new day welcome the changes, or become a new beginning for you all. Therefore, as both minutes and hours go by, your mind will constantly churn over those many decisions to be made, actions to be completed, and plans to create. Then, within the process, the core of each should contain purity of thought, which ultimately transcends and encapsulates your heart and soul.

If one should struggle with such ethics, ideals, and alterations though, then perhaps it is easier to start with the body instead. This is because it is vital that you try to keep yourself clean and healthy, and also wear fresh clothes each day. Even if you have but one set of clothes, you can remain tidy. And your teeth, too, should be cleansed of all food debris ... ideally twice a day.

I state these pretty basic things because once an individual takes care of their body; it becomes easier to bring purity into their mind. Know that your home and surroundings also portray the true you. If your home is unkempt and unclean, no matter if it's a tin shack, a shed, or made of stone or brick, then what does this say about the 'dweller'? I do not imply that one should be constantly clearing 24 hours a day, 7 days per week, but state that regular removal of dirt and bacteria can keep you healthy in more ways than one.

Indeed, it has become so easy to neglect oneself (or one's abode) because of the modern, hectic pace in which the societies of the world now live. However, all must realise it can lead to more difficult scenarios and situations later on. If one accepts an unclean environment, then it is easier for negativity and impurity to enter the mind. This then becomes a downward slope, which can also lead to unhappiness, jealousy, or even hatred.

There can be no half measures where you strive for purity. It may seem wise to try to disguise what you have said and done, like brushing dust or rubbish under a carpet, but out of sight will never mean out of mind. Such things are no different to stored karma, and through those good—or even 'Godly'—acts. One may feel that they are bringing balance and equilibrium and order from chaos, but unless action is undertaken (in whatever respect) with a purity of thought, then the resulting outcome will just become temporary. It would be like mowing the grass; it will soon have to be re-cut, no matter what level you set the blades at.

And so, the mind, body and soul are entwined, just like the Father, Son, and Holy Spirit. Again, it may seem that they are each separate, but they are not. How could they ever be? Are such sayings like, "You are what you eat", true or false? Cannot pain be felt emotionally, physically, and mentally too? Does light and love not flow through all parts of the Holy Trinity?

You need to decide these things for yourself. But any word or deed enacted with purity of thought will always result in positive energy being relayed upon—and in—many levels of vibration and dimension. This means that not only can my (yes, God's) will be done … but also the will of the 'majority'.

The latter can occur in numerous ways, though I do not state that it is guaranteed. More often than not, much can be achieved when many hearts link in prayer and truth. For example, how else can tyrants or dictatorships come to abrupt ends without the 'will' of the people?

It is important to know that the exact opposite can occur. Collective impure thoughts—which can lead to wrong action and anger—which then divide and break down true human values in society. How else can the riots and destruction in London in 2011 spread to other parts of the country so quickly? People will say because of technology and the media, but everything starts with a simple thought. Once again, the individual must decide how much impact a little piece of 'dirt' can have.

So, where are we now within this discussion and process? Do you feel and wish to pick up a tin of polish, pot of paint; sweeping brush and spring clean your home or garden? Will a change of clothes freshen up your outlook, or make people see you in a different light? Can it be that a simple … that a kind thought actually changes or helps another? Or that positive thoughts even change your life?

Please understand too, that with a prayer—if it is with the purity, sincerity, and devotion—linking heart and mind; then your thoughts can elevate above the clutter and your daily anxiety or worries and thus rise into the ether. However, some will think their thoughts can just fade or float aimlessly away. Not so. I know them all, like a mother knows her child. I feel them like a gentle embrace from loving arms, and I sense them as they attract my attention, just like a magnet.

Comprehend too that my energy is your energy; hence, true love always merges with my own. Likewise, those hearts which strive for purity and who wish to draw closer to me … by taking one step towards me, I will always take many more towards you. Do not mistake what I mean, though, for my love is still unconditional.

That said, it is very important to remember … in trying to cleanse your heart and soul's karma, it can bring both opportunities to shine and also introduce many more trials and tribulations to endure. By explaining this, one should not fear as I am always near (as I constantly reiterate). Even so, who would not wish to remove the sticky black molasses—which attempt to hide your divine spark—sooner rather than later?

As always, these choices are your own, but I urge every soul to radiate as brightly as one can or wishes to be. Realise too, you are all part of an eternal living flame, each as brilliant—and illuminating—as a thousand, or even a billion suns. Let your friends, family, and all whom you meet feel your radiance and love. If freely shared and given, it will help many others in their own endeavours, too.

So, each of you can lead by example. Not for plaudits or to satisfy or stroke the ego, because truly helping each other is as inherent within you as your own DNA. To ignore any other beings' plight or pain is not a chromosome deficiency, or so-called birth defect or disability. No, those choices are from an ill-conceived character and personality; selfish, unloving and in denial of one's true purpose and goal.

For a soul's growth and to become cleansed, the thoughts that emanate from deep within you need to become selfless, unsullied by material or sensual desires. As stated before, I do not mean you have to give away or live with no possessions or comforts, or that one should become celibate. It is only those attachments which lead you to being—or feeling—discontent, for they now need to become detached; left behind like a shadow.

When you believe and step forward even more into the light, you'll be working in truth, and then your life will change beyond recognition. This will give new meaning to your working days and a new purpose to life. For all that's said and done, you can still decide to stay on the same course as you think you are right now.

Know that I always love you. I love you all. So, whether you believe you are living in a nightmare scenario, or think that you're in paradise, trust in the love that is deep inside your heart. It is here and here alone that you will hear my call and my direction. It will never fail you. When all seems lost or beyond your control, you will receive the answers you need. So, not only trust in me, but trust in yourself, too.

By recognizing and understanding our union, you will have gained self–realization and, therefore, wipe the slate clean. The lines and traces of any broken promises, faded dreams, hurt, or pain can be erased, leaving only the ability to re-write one's own future into eternity. It is that pure and that simple. Amen.

LESSON 15:
FACT OR FICTION

Welcome to another lesson. I hope you will feel it inside your heart, with its message also becoming etched beyond your mind ... to both touch and guide you deep within your soul.

Okay, please understand that just as the rain and wind obscure the view from the window, they start to resemble both the tears and the breathless sighs which befall the many—and who are still uncertain of what is real and what is not. Indeed, throughout the life of every person, all will experience such times of uncertainty, not knowing fact from fiction, which brings doubt or even fear.

So, once again, I ask you how you feel at this present moment. Are you strengthened by your current religious beliefs? If so, has your own faith become stronger now than it was before? Know that difficult times bring darkened clouds to countless doors and hearts, which can restrict one's vision further, but only if you accept them, in the belief they have a very real hold over you. Thus, those stresses and strains, and much anxiety, can inhibit those positive thoughts and energy which wish to soar both far and wide.

If you can only see them as temporary moments within your life, these situations will surely come and go ... just like the passing rain clouds, which seemed to have slowed down and hovered over you. I promise you they will fade and disappear. So, remember, every cloud has a silver lining. Simply stop and look and listen right now, because birds sweetly sing their merry tunes, and a blue sky emerges as if by some magical feat or trick.

Sometimes you may see a rainbow—or be fortunate to witness a double rainbow—which highlights both vibration and energy, resonating through a spectrum of colour. After a while, its natural beauty may seem to lose definition, because the 'conditions' required for it to be displayed 'change', though this is not unlike your heart, is it not?

Undeniably, you can also drift from positive thoughts and actions to those of mistrust, impatience, and frustration. The shine of your own radiance becomes sullied, glowing like a candlelight behind frosted glass. But what does your heart tell you of this situation? How important is it really, other than to yourself, or even to those who bear witness to how you look, and what you say, think, or do?

Are you being true to yourself in how you live your life? Should you now behave differently to meet the expectations of others? If so, they might think, 'That can't be you'. Does your wife, husband, partner, or lover know or understand the 'real' you? Or do you live life on automatic pilot, becoming what others require or wish you to be?

Therefore, realise foremost, it is your own responsibility to believe and trust in yourself. This is a fact. So too, is the reality that once you do this, you will also trust and then believe in me.

Try to dismiss those thoughts that you are just a body. This is fiction. Likewise, so is the notion that you are a body which has a soul. No, you are love and light, a spark of divinity, a soul that sought embodiment to balance —or clear—your own karmic 'debt', and to experience and grow and to love.

Again, this highlights the unique opportunity for each one of you to erase and eradicate the imbalance within this very lifetime. 51% of past ill thoughts, words, and deeds removed will see that your ascension takes place. The other 49%—as I have often stated—can be worked through, upon, and within the higher octaves of love and light, if so required. Again, this is truth, a fact, and not fiction.

So, what can one do to help you overcome such difficulties and therefore take advantage of a so-called 'spiritual amnesty'? Well, you can try to keep things simple where your thoughts and words and deeds. Simplicity is the key to practically every aspect of your life. Therefore, while your mind tries to complicate matters, giving reasons both for and against almost every aspect of living, your heart can be pushed to one side and almost discarded as being irrelevant. Of course, this is far from the truth, but to discuss it here could make another 'lesson'—or a story—all of its own.

With this said, I would now like you to recognize the authenticity of your dreams. Through them, many people experience spiritual awakenings, or even visitations of love, in its countless forms. For example, if you were to hear, see, or sense any religious figurehead or Godhead, such as Jesus, Sai Baba, Krishna, or Mohammed ... then you must appreciate this is as real as if you were meeting them during your waking hours.

The expression 'Spirit does not waste' comes to the fore. If one is fortunate to receive light and truth this way, then they have been truly blessed with my grace. Afterwards—upon waking up—it is down to the individual to decide whether the dream (or vision) was real 'life'. Or, if it was all hocus-pocus, unrelated and even dismissed by stating something like, "I only had this dream, because I ate cheese too late in the evening!"

But if they weren't real, how could one leave their body upon the bed, to experience the reality on another plane, in a different time, or dimension? So, comprehend that this is a double-edged sword. Whether something is black or white, light, or dark, or fact or fiction … it is all in the 'I' of the beholder. Remember, only when your heart, soul, and mind are 'one', then true vision is obtained.

By any other method, everything is an illusion. When the eyes of the body work alone; you can only witness the impermanent world which relays uncertainty, confusion, and discontent. I ask you, therefore, if the world in which you live can become glorified, would one still desire and wish to sleep in more than one bed, drive many cars, own several properties, or travel between continents morning, noon, and night?

Of course not. So once again, you need to perceive where the reality and facts start, and where negativity and lies end. When you come back to basics, the way ahead will become easier to tread. Truth illuminates the pathway, as those correct decisions will make every Sun go down on the horizon. Has it disappeared for good? Do you fear it will not rise the next morning? No … you take it as fact.

Likewise, with the Moon, when you see its effects upon the sea's tide, would you believe the waves have evaporated into thin air and never returned to the shore? No … because you take it as a fact too. On a lesser scale, with those living in the 'modern' world, when you flick a light switch and nothing happens, aren't you more shocked and concerned? Yes, you probably are … because you would expect an immediate illumination of your surroundings.

Well, those within the 'spirit realms', drawing close to each, are no less shocked to witness someone who appears to wander around in the darkness. It can often resemble a person who just waits and waits and waits, believing that someone else will lead the way for them, "Why use my light when I can use someone else's?" But this is like the blind leading the blind.

You all need to play your own part within the home, neighbourhood, and society with the understanding you are each as important as each other. So, do not strive to better oneself through ego, jealousy, or pride. Indeed, these all form negative traits. They misdirect the person and soul to either fade or wane with fear, or fuel anger with hatred and desire … and both are causes of internal and external stress and 'dis-ease'.

Therefore, by helping one another whenever and wherever you can, not only does the positive energy and vibration resonate at higher frequencies within you, but you also uplift the very same of those where your support is given too. All are 'one', remember.

Overall, in reading or hearing these words—just like any other book—the individual must ultimately deem whether they are fact or fiction. Perhaps they will mean nothing to some and everything to another? To the 'masses' … they may even fall somewhere in between. However, once infused into the psyche, only goodness and light will shine.

It is not brainwashing. It is your heart's cleansing that I seek to assist you in, and the same for every soul. As always, it is only you who can—and will—decide, for I will never use force or any coercion.

I love you all. My heart is yours for all eternity. Know this too, you are already free. This can become a reality in the world … as all will seek eternal bliss and peace in me. If you can understand this lesson, you will also comprehend this is truly fact, and not fiction. Amen.

LESSON 16:

CALLING

When you become still and drift into quietness, true peace and energy descend upon the physical, both within and out. Your heart rate will slow down. The inner sense and ability to send—and also receive love—then knows no bounds. Only in this moment can you hear me calling you. I hope you will recognize my voice, urging you to let go of all the negativity and apprehension which clings like ivy upon a tree.

In this stillness, you can understand the difference between the exterior world—with its influences and impermanent desires—and the true creation where bliss and love reign supreme. Therefore, in your hectic life, one must ask if you actually betray yourself. Are you making up reasons or excuses not to connect with your own heart?

Are you too busy or too stressed? Perhaps with home, family, or even work issues to be sorted out, as you attempt to control them all? Or do you try to honour the beauty and the perfection inside of you by really listening to what I relay and share through our eternal link, which can never be broken? Remember, if you can remove the external clutter which emanates from the mind, then everything becomes clearer and easier for you to understand. This will help you become more focused, whilst giving you a platform of strength to work from.

Indeed, not only would you be less concerned about unimportant things, but you'd realise that by going with the flow, you'll also worry less about those decisions you feel must be made there and then. It is as if they were vital to your safety and for your own—or another's—well-being. I do not mean (or encourage) you to take a backseat here, and simply let the world go by. But if you can place your trust in the choices you make, and not think, "I should have done this or that instead", your life will be much easier to bear.

Once you can 'accept'—which means having the acceptance of what life reveals to you every day—you do not need to worry about tomorrow, next week, next month, or year. Can you believe all is as it should be; no matter if your current situation has bestowed fear, joy, pain, laughter, or sadness at your door? If you can, then not only do you trust yourself, but it confirms that you trust in me implicitly.

Do you think I can make mistakes? If the answer is no, then why do you ever worry, feel anxious, or cast doubt upon and into the ether? As there are so many miracles around you all the time, where can the illusion and confusion come from? Can you not hear 'nature' through the window? Are not love, light, and truth being displayed constantly for each of you to survey?

Please appreciate, I am the songs from those birds who are communicating with each other. I am the owl, crow, fox, and all elements of life that call to their young. They teach, guide, and support them until they are ready to understand how to live, and become 'detached'. So too, by listening and hearing your own inner voice, you can leave the earthly abode —which you feel is 'home'—and fly to where you truly belong. Like a classroom of life, you'll soon want to spread your wing to fly with me. Know that I am your other wing to help you scale new heights to live eternally within my heart.

Please do not feel or be mistaken that you will need to go or travel somewhere. One does not need to find the secrets of bliss and peace in faraway places. Nor feel as though they are being kept under lock and key, which you're unable to receive or access. This cannot be. You only need to realise that everything is there already, both inside and out of you.

Also, do not imagine that I will disconnect you, like an operator on an exchange line. I do not ask for 50 cents (pence, yen, or any other currency) more, to still communicate with me. I never 'charge' you to feel part of me. All that I am is yours. This is why I keep reiterating that you all form creation. How can you need or require anything else when you already have it all?

What you can do though—if you think it will be of some benefit or help your cause—is to reverse these illusionary, pretend, and so-called charges. Remember, by installing your trust in me, I will take up all the burdens from your body, heart, and soul. I shall never miss—or not answer—your calls, even though so many believe that I do.

Listen, when someone pleads with me, offering their heart and soul for me to help them, or perhaps ask me to save a loved one from danger or deep peril, it can seem that I do not care. Or, that I did not hear the call … was otherwise engaged, assuming I was somewhere else. But no, this is never the case. Not only do I hear the call, I know what their loved one needs in their own life, of what karma is being cleared or balanced, and every reason, too.

So, can you comprehend now that I do not make mistakes? Even when you are seeing unbelievable acts of 'man versus man', and 'man versus nature', I am the universal witness and 'I' of truth. The scales of justice within earthly courts may seem trivial or even bizarrely unjust to some, but all must comprehend that there is no secret which can be kept from me.

In all that's said and done, one may still believe I sit upon a throne, to raise my hand and place a thumb up or down, but no. Because, as I keep repeating, you are each your own judge and jury ... for every soul—deep within—truly wishes to feel and share love. Therefore, once departed from the 'earth-plane', one will fully realise and sense all the hurt that has been caused, and all the joy and happiness in which you have shared, too.

Once understood, every soul instinctively wishes to help repair and make amends where needed. Therefore, it can take many lifetimes to succeed. However, within this lifetime, you all have the chance to fast track towards the truth and light, both with—and through—my grace, which I have given upon you.

As stated upon many occasions, through self-realization, you immediately come to terms with whom and what you are, and why you exist. Therefore, karmic imbalance and debt are more easily removed. Even those past deeds which may seem immovable—being strongly bound to you like granite—will all eventually be removed. They will become washed away by tears of joy, far more powerful than water eroding rock.

So, while these earthly years contain both highs and lows, it is vital you treat them with indifference. It is all 'experience'. This subsequently turns knowledge into wisdom. And, alongside an unbendable faith of your chosen religion, or in one handed down to you by your forbearers ... if it portrays and exists on peace and love, it cannot fail to highlight the 'oneness' of creation, and our true eternal connection.

Know, too, that your heart is my heart. As an undying flame of light, you are each entrusted to shine and illuminate as brightly as you can. Not because I request or would ever demand it, but because you yourself wish to honour and upheld your own spark of divinity. This also helps to reveal the path for those just starting their journey too. Or for those who have lost their way, having deviated from the pathway of their own truth.

As always, I will help you achieve and meet your goals, and true desires of love and light. Though 'needs' must constantly come before 'wants'. Finally, should uncertainty or doubt ever try to confuse or misguide you, know that I am here always, and forever will be. So ... can you hear me calling? Amen.

LESSON 17:
TEST

From before the moment of your birth into physical embodiment, you will have trials and tribulations to deal with and overcome. These are only situations or events to help you grow as a human being and soul. How you deal with—and more importantly—how you accept them; will show your spiritual development and growth as a soul and spark of Divinity.

However, please note that you have the same equal chance—and the choice—to test what you receive from any source of help, whether it is through the physical, mental, or emotional aspects of your being. Therefore, if the spiritual guidance and education can be heard or read—or in any way touches your senses—you may establish whether it is just, and good, and if it comes to, through, or by you in the name of love and light.

For a moment, try to cast your mind back to biblical times and the Lord's 40 days between his resurrection and ascension. Did Thomas not have his 'doubt' removed by placing his hand and fingers into and upon Christ's wounds? Jesus wanted—and also needed him—to have his proof, so it would become part of his story (history), which unfolded to leave all souls upon the 'earth-plane' with the same task to believe, and therefore 'live'.

Now, in this modern age, what will make each of you continue to believe and grow? What evidence will a person require to understand their life and true purpose? For some, nothing is necessary. For others, perhaps even love —which can glisten and shine like a beacon within a darkened room—is still not enough. The truth can't be seen as the heart, and 'I', pretend to be divided.

Please comprehend that it is good to question (and also test) every source where guidance is requested. Remember, too, within all dimensions of time and space, no element of light can ever be offended. So, do not be afraid or at all worried by continually asking for confirmation if that is what you need.

As so many of you are working upon different levels—which does not make someone better than another in any way, shape, or form—a soul may recognize me and my love within any form of life. Others, meanwhile, may feel the truth via dreams, visions, or by gazing upon natural (or even unnatural) phenomena which materialize within the impermanent world where you live.

Perhaps it is being a witness to a solar eclipse, the northern lights, shooting stars, or even a comet which can help one question or believe they are part of something far greater than themselves. Therein lays the clue which I often reiterate. It is through your own self-realization you will obtain bliss and peace. I can simplify this even further still, which is to simply 'know thyself'.

You will know what 'truth' is at all times because it will resonate inside you. When the answer you seek—and the illumination and guidance you need seem to click and just fall into place—within mind, heart, and soul, it will feel natural. You do not need to force yourself. Nor fight against how you feel to make something both understandable and meaningful. So, let life come to you. Try to approach each day with zest and zeal, not with dread, anguish, or uncertainty. This way, you can see time as less of a test and more of an opportunity to become a shining example of who you really are.

Armed with this knowledge, you can move forward with a conviction that all is well and as it should be. No need to fret, with thoughts you should do something else, or that you have not achieved what your mind insists you could have done.

Indeed, the world around you constantly judges or looks to criticize the results of someone's deeds or actions. People forget to see the effort in the part one may have played. Is it really about getting success and winning all the time, whereby 2nd place or being part of the so-called 'also-rans' becomes a crime?

Know that each of you has abilities. Some are unique in different fields and in diverse ways. As per character and make-up, the body may have many types of personality, but within you are all divine. Not everyone has to strive to be the best in the world, as you are all 'stars' to me.

Practice does not always make perfect. To enforce or place pressure of any kind can prove very harmful, especially to the young. This, of course, is not the same as encouragement, discipline, and endeavour, which are all traits one can either accept or not.

A mother or father who wishes to see their offspring rise to the top of a profession or skill is fine, but the test is not theirs. Hence, the child's desire for success may not always be the same as their own. What is important is that life's tests are for each and for all.

I have stated frequently that I am not your judge or jury, for you are each your own. As such, do I therefore wish for you to witness the truth? Of course, I do. Would I rather you understand and have faith in the real and true 'you', reaching ascension in this lifetime, instead of continual rebirth and death … absolutely.

I AM I The Indweller of Your Heart—Book Three

So, please realise that you are the very gift of love which wishes to express itself. Through angels, saints, and my presence among you all, I have already shown you the way. Jesus stated you are all made in my image —your divinity—so how many years (or lifetimes) does it take for the penny to drop? This is not criticism, as it would be like chastising and criticizing my 'self' as I am I! No, these are only words on a page. It is always down to you to decide what to do with the time you have been given.

Understand, by taking a backward step, you will actually take more than one step forward, but how, and what do I mean? Well, as discussed, many times before, when you trust yourself, you must therefore also trust me. That being the case, appreciate that I am working through you. You are not constantly the 'do-er'. This doesn't get you off the proverbial hook, but means that if you can allow your hands to be mine, your thoughts to be my thoughts, and so on and so forth, only 'good' will ensue.

If you can believe I am in you, and am also within your friend, neighbour, and family members, wouldn't you always try to be and do your best? Hence, by serving through your work, rest, and play within society, you are also serving me. And, if you should feel something has gone wrong, the result turning out to someone's disapproval, I will then accept all consequences as my burden, not yours.

Please know, you truly have to believe and make the effort in what you do, though. Half-hearted gestures of goodwill, or to make the result for one's own gain, only continues—or worsens—Karmic imbalance. Therefore—and ultimately within this process—the world can indeed become a much brighter, cleaner, safer place when all souls lose their selfishness, replacing it with selflessness.

And so, what events or tasks have you completed today? Did they test your mind, body, or even perhaps your heart? Could you have said, acted, or thought in a more positive way? Was there an opportunity to help someone or something less fortunate than you? Appreciate that life can be as beautiful and as glorious as you wish to make it. It makes no difference where, or in what skin, you are born. If you can live with and through good conduct, peace, love, and truth, then your own life can glow and become amazingly colourful.

Everyone has a choice, though some do 'experience' more often than others. Likewise, there will always be those who 'have', and there will always be the 'have-nots', but the Sun warms and shines upon every face just the same. Likewise, a smile and laughter also transcend any language or continent, plane, or dimension.

The ultimate test cannot be swapped or exchanged, bargained for, or given away. It is each your very own. All have love inside them. This is a fact. As I have explained before, even a madman loves someone or something. Believe I am within and with you always—so take and pass the test—and in simply knowing yourself ... and you will find you're already there. Amen.

LESSON 18:
CLOTHES

I have spoken recently about the importance of keeping the clothes that you wear clean, because it reflects from, through, and upon the 'inner' self. I therefore wish to expand upon this area today for one's growth and greater awareness.

So, it has often been said that clothes 'maketh' the man, somehow depicting and placing the person into a 'pigeon-hole' of character and personality. But how much truth is there in this? Some people may also assume that those wearing a business suit are probably intelligent, have honourable professions, are financially well off—or are wealthy. Perhaps it might even be all three.

For many others, though, one's education and appearance can hide both good and positive traits. And evil and negative ones too, just like a wolf in sheep's clothing. Therefore, do clothes actually make the man? Well, each one of you may have different viewpoints, so there can often be 'truth' on each side of the story.

For instance, some would state you can judge a person and their character by the condition of what they wear, and the shoes upon their feet. But, if they are scuffed, unclean, and unpolished, do you think this might also depict their attitude to life—or even their soul—as an unkempt or even an unloved one?

In contrast, could (or would) you deem the homeless, a vagrant or so-called tramp, to be any less concerned with their own heart and soul than another's, simply because they seem to be this way about their hair or appearance? In fact, there are many more elements or sides to this scenario. You could even say it is multi-faceted. It not only incorporates opinions but must also include the circumstances and reason behind self-discipline, self-neglect, and even one's health.

By understanding that a 'down and out' may have pure light and love flowing through their veins, all hearts shine and can illuminate and guide others from a pathway of tears. Therefore, is it too easy to judge and quickly condemn another with prejudicial views, which have themselves been cast upon the mind by ego, disdain, frustration, jealousy, or pride?

To thrive and continually grow as part of humanity, one must display tolerance and forgiveness in equal measure. In addition, offering encouragement and kindness, not only beyond the physical expression of materialism ... but also emotionally and mentally too. One's strength does not just encapsulate the body. Know that it also represents and brings stamina to the mind and fortitude of the heart.

Now then, it is easy to assume that this lesson will teach and explain from the viewpoint of just clothing the skin, but what about your soul covered by the body? This is your first exterior garment or 'overcoat' after all. Well, the body is both amazing and beautiful, isn't it? Though how often do you stop to contemplate this? Perhaps hardly ever ... unless your health is compromised—or that of a relative or friend—because it is so often taken for granted. Not until it suffers aches and pains, becomes ill through neglect, abuse, or overwork (constantly pushed beyond its limits), does one realise how important, how valuable, and how fragile it can be.

Of course, from the very moment of your physical birth, the body is aging. Only through a continual effort to maintain it can it cope with the interior and exterior rain of tears, frozen hearts, and the pressure and turbulence of—and from—the mind. This resembles strong gales attempting to knock you off of your feet.

So, how can you have additional protection whenever such troubled times come? Well, your faith can be your umbrella. It shall act like a shield, not only against another's thoughts and feelings—which would like to penetrate your mind—but also stop you wishing to do just the same. Understand your trust will ensure that the overcoat will function as it should. It will insulate you through and against 'bitter' enemies from within.   And also when worldly desires whirl and whip up into a frenzied chill of discontent. Then, your own inner belief will enable you to know the truth of why you must prevail, and of who and what you truly can become.

Know each of these elements can fasten down any entry of doubt that wishes to test you—trying to discover whether you are prepared or not. Similarly, like three amazing buttons, the mind, heart, and soul are stronger when fully functioning as 'one'. Perhaps, your God—I am I—can also be seen as a 'fail-safe'. Consider me a protective zip or a fast solution if (or when) you need some extra support to keep negativity, fear, or despair away from you both quickly and effectively.

I watch over all of you. Therefore, I know some of your garments (bodies) are new. Others, meanwhile, hang together by threads of hope. Each one of you has a 'sell-by' date, which your own soul has chosen. Only through karma and my grace can it ever be changed. This is only if 'love' requires or demands it to be done. How else could a loved one actually live beyond the time which medically should have come and gone?

Yes indeed, love knows no bound. You must understand the same. When a child—who comes into the physical world—lives for only one second, one minute, or just one hour. The souls of all concerned know what they need and not what is wanted, however painful it appears to be.

Now then, let me ask you, do you look after yourself? Truly, do you? Do you ever question what or how much you eat or exercise? Does the thought of cleanliness next to godliness ever cross your mind? Well, after all is said and done, perhaps it is not the body which needs looking after first, but perhaps it is the mind? How often would you look at yourself and let your mind dictate whether your clothes and/or body suit you? Alternatively, could the opinions of others become more important than the acceptance of yourself, deep within your own heart?

I urge you, please, do not succumb to such things as negativity likes to rip holes into the fabric of your well-being. It does this by picking away at your positive thinking, believing that it will cause non-repairable damage to your self-confidence. But I am the 'I' of the needle, which is your very real and first defence, working and mending tirelessly, not on your behalf, but with you, together as one.

So, there are many similarities between the clothes of your body and the cloth of your soul. Ultimately, it is always your own choice to establish if one is more than—or as equally important as—the other.

Eventually, when it is time to leave the mortal coil, the soul will elevate beyond the weight of exterior garments. Hopefully, it will have done its job, enabling you to experience not only the clearing and balancing of karmic debt but also the wonder of 'embodiment' which has enabled you to express your love and kindness beyond both the body and mind.

From this day forward, may your thoughts bring a fresh beginning, like wearing new shoes which shine with every step you take … so the heart can welcome the enlightened path of truth that you now walk upon. Amen.

LESSON 19:

CAMOUFLAGE

Can you see, feel, hear, or sense me this very minute, hour, day, week, month, or year? Do you imagine I am hiding from you, deep within a secret enclave, being witnessed or becoming known only to a select few? Am I so distant, far away, over hills, valleys, or seas, and out of sight or mind, and away from your heart?

Of course not. So, in the way you live, act, and even breathe, can you really believe you are alone, separate, and with an imaginable boundary or fence made of hardened attitudes or beliefs that has been erected in a desperate attempt to shut me out? Can anyone also think that so-called good or bad deeds can actually camouflage the truth and effulgence of their own divinity?

Appreciate that I am with all souls. Therefore, unlike a chameleon which can blend in with its surroundings, to even attempt to disguise one's own thoughts, words, or actions from me is pointless. It would be a waste of your time, precious energy, and love. Please realise, though, I am not the spy camera or a 'big brother' but am the 'I' of truth within you and without, above and below, in front and behind you, too. I am your conscience and your intuition, and the petals and plumes of your radiating heart, which bloom with a perfume and fragrance of our love as one.

As such, what would seem to highlight and resonate more so within the ether, time, and space? Is it one's hurt, anger, and pain? Or is it perhaps compassion, truth, and forgiveness? Also, are any of the elements of thought, word, and deed more—or less—powerful than each other? Do you believe negativity, hate, and darkness are more powerful than positive energy, radiating both love and light?

By now, all should comprehend that love is the strongest energy and force within all creation. In reality, this is only often recognized when it overcomes, diffuses, or transcends those times when a person or soul thinks they can no longer 'control' a situation, or think they are alone. During such times, it can seem as if I have been hiding behind a darkened screen, deceiving you of what you had hoped to see, feel, think ,or believe would happen or come true.

Please know this is, was, and never will be the case. Time and time again, those instances occur only because of the imaginary barrier the mind has placed between us. It implies and wants to insist you can cope with all that life throws at you. And that you are doing everything yourself (alone) without me being involved at all.

I understand that upon the physical realm, this aspect of human nature comes into being because it is much easier to think you are 'body' first. This, of course, is not the case. The energy of the 'mind' also wishes to disguise many hearts from me. It tries to insist that you are all separate bodies, being divided by colour, creed, or religion. But why would it do this, and for what purpose? And for whose benefit?

Some will argue or state, "Well, you're God, so why don't you just sort it out … along with everything else that seems wrong within the world?" This is an interesting viewpoint, not least because if just one person follows this train of thought, then they have indeed grown spiritually and developed in both heart and soul.

'How?' … you ask. Well, as with all education and knowledge, only through experience can you gain wisdom. Hence, having belief—and each spark of divinity knowing thy 'self—can only be accomplished by overcoming the false separateness, which this notion had implied. It can be as powerful, or as weak, as the very 'thought' is allowed to be.

The mind is consciousness and energy. And being part of all creation—is as valuable or as irresponsible as you encourage it to become. It can make one feel it has all the answers. Its goodness lies in the fact it will always attempt to protect your overall well-being. That said, its weakness is in pretending to provide the soul with options and guidance, giving the seeker the belief, it has the correct and only way forward to lead and guide you. But the mind only ever bases its reasoning and judgment upon the past, and therefore, real truth is camouflaged.

Here lies the test between mind and heart. You may need to instruct and pose the questions to the mind, but it is within the heart where the answers lay sleeping, awaiting the call and the awakening for truth.

So where do you go from here? Well, one's intuition, those gut feelings are discussed elsewhere, and therefore do not need a further explanation at this time. Remember, only you can truly decide this. It is you who can state whether you're feeling happy and fulfilled, or still searching for perpetual bliss within the material world in which your soul currently resides.

People often state that they feel there is something missing, but they do not know or understand what it is. Realise this will never be found in a new car, a house, or anything made within the impermanent plane. However, as there is that chink of light, or if you hear the one voice of truth within the stillness which beckons, you might believe there is so much more to your current situation and life.

The assumed 'missing' ingredient is only the recognition of our connection. No more, or any less than this. So, with the aid of these books, and from the light within, you can steer through the emotional waters of life. Although one must experience the peaks and troughs of their own path, those who have acknowledged the divinity in all will traverse these with equanimity, bringing both balance and meaning to their past, present, and future.

Accept too, anxiety, fear and uncertainty are all traits of the masks which hide the fact that one currently cannot trust in oneself, and in me. It is nearly always self-inflicted, because ultimately each one of you needs to acknowledge your destiny and the responsibility of your own soul. You can only complete your goal of ascension through self-realization. You can lead a horse to water, but you cannot make it drink … remember.

This, of course, is different to love, as unconditional love is limitless. It cannot be contained or restricted … and has no bounds. Overall, by staying focused and having an open heart will ensure you will become your own eternal witness to the truth. The worldly desires which camouflage this—and slow you down in the process—must be seen with the heart, mind, and soul in unison to enable true insight to take place.

With patience and perseverance, you will distinguish any disguise, as it always moves, alters, or falls. Subsequently, you can separate the wheat from the chaff to make correct decisions and choices, which not only affect yourself, but those who are close around you.

It is important to make sure that you are always portraying the real you. You can never maintain your life by living or walking in someone else's shoes, with another's standards or beliefs. This can devastate, like living an eternal lie, because it has the power to destroy the serenity, peace, and calmness which are truly yours inside.

The ugliest mask of all is deceit, because even if looked upon through rose-coloured glasses, the 'truth will always out'. There are no secrets that can be kept from me. Even if one believes the hands of time will make it fade or hide—by being buried under layers of illusion—and even when one 'dies', the truth still remains.

So, be seen as who you really are. You may have been given a 'name' upon the Earth, but in truth you are 'Atma' … which is love, the 'I am I', and the God in me 'is'. No bodily garment can ever disguise, mask, or camouflage this fact. It can only ever temporarily hide it from one another. Know right now that every soul will permanently discard this veil of misapprehension upon their ascension. Amen.

LESSON 20:
PORTAL

As I have explained many times before, everything is from, through, and to the heart. Our connection is permanent. When you become still, all the answers you seek reside there. And so, your education now continues. But do you feel it is only—or entirely—of this world? Or can you grow and learn elsewhere, too?

When you're deep in meditation (which is no more than the release of desire and attachment), are you awake, asleep, or perhaps even somewhere in between? Try to understand, by removing the process of 'thought' from the mind, you become detached from the limitations of time and distance, or dimension.

Over many eras, people have pondered the stars and galaxies above. All the while trying to establish how to link or reach beyond them ... attempting to comprehend possible modes of transport, and the effects it would have upon the body and mind. However, this contains its own problem and shortfalls. In trying to expand the capacity of the mind, this actually decreases the ability to learn how to fly ... beyond the boundary of the senses.

What do I mean by this? Well, let me ask you, what takes place when you dream? Before you try to consider this, you must fully recognize that souls in the embodiment of 'man', such as Carl Jung and Sigmund Freud, documented and organized many worthwhile facts of the unconscious, sleep, and dream states. Nevertheless, I wish to simplify such evaluations for you.

Now then, imagine yourself asleep right now. You are within a dream, perhaps across the other side of the world, upon a different planet or even in a celestial heaven. Ask yourself, how did I get there? Was there a machine or vehicle with special fuel placed in its 'tank'? Had angels—or maybe demons—elevated you upon their wings and carried you across or through the depths of space? Perhaps you believe they did.

Could you have walked through a gateway or portal which links this world with another? Did you then require so-called alien technology to break free from the gravitational pull of the Earth and of your earthly 'body'?

Please remember something that I have stated many times before ... that you are already free. This being the case, all one needs to do is to go beyond the mind and one's restrictive thoughts. During stillness or deep sleep, your soul does not need to think of how to be somewhere, it just is. How amazing, how 'one-derful' is that?

So, the mind always attempts to reason and justify. This grounds the soul with a real or imaginary ball and chain. In effect, one is anchored to—and left angered with—the physical, by this heavy umbilical cord made up from frustration and despair. Each is a repetitive 'link' in the desire to make the unknown ... known. In comparison, when you trust and let go of preconceived ideas on exactly how to experience such beauty within the realms of creation, the differences will become quite clear.

It is the higher 'self' which is your means to experience the different levels of consciousness, and those layers of vibration/energy are therefore the true portal. These cannot be seen with physical eyes alone. It is love that contains the umbilical cord of truth and which connects your soul to me. The closest word you may use to describe it is that it is 'crystallized' in appearance.

Therefore, one does not have constraints of time or distance. They are only relevant where such boundaries are required to exist and assist you in the lower, denser vibration/energies where your body resides. This is proved by recalling your own dreams. When deep within the 'experience', you are never concerned—or have the need to look for a clock—as you no longer fear missing or have the passing of 'time', do you?

Whatever the occurrence, vision, or dream, you precisely return the moment I mean you to. This may seem like 1 second or even 1 hour when you re-awake or become cognizant of your earthbound surroundings. You are (and can be) grounded in the blink of an eye/'I'.

Coming back down to Earth now ... imagine you are looking at a gateway. For some, this maybe appear wooden, feeling natural (nature), while for others it might be metal (manmade) ...or it might just resemble an open door (spiritual). What do you feel lurks or lies behind it? Is it a secret garden? If so, will it be cultivated, tended to by those internal aspirations for growth and oneness? Or are the very thoughts of negativity and possessiveness of the body smothering you like weeds, restricting you from taking flight?

In reality, you have now taken up this inner fight. Otherwise, you would not be where you are now ... and actually reading or hearing these words. So, this is good. You realize it and recognize you are so very much more than the body.

Know and believe then, that you can eradicate all things which cling and cover the soil—and soul—through being thorough and meticulous with the seeds that you sow. Only by sharing peace, love, and kindness will these spread and join like a patchwork quilt, covering the ground and path you walk upon, ensuring only those good things will grow and flourish. Sometimes this may seem very difficult, but many hands make 'light' work. Just like a magnet, you will draw and be drawn to like-minded and like hearted souls.

As a result, you not only do your 'spiritual' work upon the physical plane, but you can also do so upon the ethereal planes which are as close to your divine essence as the clothes upon your body—being that the body is wrapped around the soul.

These realms are not just a portal for pleasurable experiences. They also provide the opportunity to clear karma and help other souls. This may involve rescue work, providing much needed support and help to those souls who have faded into shadow, or who have fallen into darkness. Sometimes the reverse is true. It is you who needs guidance … perhaps from angelic energies within my light hierarchy, to help you make the right decisions and actions here upon the 'earth-plane.'

Overall, I hope this lesson today has given you food for thought. Indeed, some additional nourishment for your heart which will forever wish to expand its radiance and glory. There is so very much more to digest, but like everything else, all must pass through you at the appropriate moment. The truth will flow like water in a sieve, unhindered and free. Likewise, everything which does not resonate within you cannot penetrate and disturb either your mind or heart, and we can then place it to one side.

Appreciate that this sieve is your discernment. It works in the name of love and light, and with an open heart, it will never fail you. You will know what feels, or does not feel, 'right'. You will have realised there is a unique difference between your earthly and true spiritual education, whether you undertake it on the Earth, or upon—and within—the ethereal realms.

Perhaps you already understand too that there is no material cost to you. You do not need to save for this further education. No one needs to beg, steal, or borrow. Remember, you are all entitled to know the truth, and it is both within and out, and everywhere in creation.

All have the choice to stay grounded, though some may call it the daily grindstone. But I finally explain here … you can take flight anytime, day or night. You require no ticket to pass through any gate or portal. So, why not come and fly with me … beyond the world, beyond those dreams, and into your true reality? Amen.

LESSON 21:
CONFERENCE

Welcome—as always—to all hearts that are open to receive and send love … whenever and wherever they may be. Indeed, no matter the plane or dimension you reside upon, love resonates and transcends both time and distance. It bathes the soul with peace and goodwill, bound with faith and hope.

Please understand, the soul and your divine essence (in its one true desire to shine and illuminate far beyond itself) require both the heart and the mind to stay open, to be strong and communicate with each other in truth. You could say that they need to be singing from the same 'hymn' sheet, and once you—as the body—accept this, then self-realization becomes easier.

However, like many disagreements and debates between people, countries, and nations, this is not always the case. Sometimes, it is just as well to lay all the cards on the table and, by coming together in a clearer, more defined, and mutual way—not to just co-exist—all should be able to progress in harmony as 'one'.

Having just mentioned such occurrences, these believed differences of thoughts and words and deeds of 'man'—over land, money, or even religious faiths across the world—can drive further wedges between you all. This makes the path and road of just one soul—or of those travelled upon by the millions—much more difficult and hazardous than it ever needs or ought to be.

As this is so, everything begins with taking care of who you are and of what you say, think, and do. As stated before, if you try to be the best human being you can be, then only goodness emanates from and also back to you. Like a ripple caused by a stone thrown into a pond, the energy always radiates outwards, but the same force (usually unseen) returns inward, too.

Therefore, how must one conduct oneself? What should be said (or unsaid) when thoughts and feelings impact upon you, seemingly threatening your well-being or your surroundings? Well, to highlight such issues, I wish for you to focus on an example, which actually encompasses three different people or so-called viewpoints, instead of only one. But how would this actually workout or illustrate what I mean? Well, just think for a moment about the heart, then the mind, and the soul.

I AM I The Indweller of Your Heart—Book Three

Imagine all three are now sitting around a table. Who wishes to start the discussion? Who might like to play the joker, and what element of 'self' feels that they should be in charge of proceedings? Like the three wise monkeys—perhaps contemplating in deep silence and darkness—will there be no talk of evil, no trace of ego to be heard, and no sleight of hand witnessed? Let truth illuminate this conference, this coming together in unison, and let's see what, in fact, materializes.

Soul: So, who wants to start then?

Mind: Thought you'd say something first!

Heart: Please, let's all be civil about this. Surely, we must trust each other.

Mind: Well, that's easy for you to say. I have to control everything, each moment of every day.

Soul: You only think you have to. Why can't you listen to the heart more often?

Mind: Hang on; I'm only trying to do my job here. If I don't attempt to reason everything, well … heart will just get upset.

Heart: No, I won't. I understand you try to look after me, but I don't believe that you always know best.

Mind: Why's that then?

Heart: Well, you always believe that if something's happened before that it will happen again. Isn't that where you always base all your advice from … the past?

Soul: That's so true. You know you do.

Mind: Wow, you're both ganging up on me here. If it wasn't for me, more often than not, you'd both be in big trouble!

Soul: Okay, we know you are trying to protect us both; we never dispute that Heart, do we?

Heart: No, I agree.

I AM I The Indweller of Your Heart—Book Three

Soul: So, then, we at least agree on something at last. Now let me ask you both a question. What do you want right now?

Heart: That's easy. I want 'love'! To feel, share, know, and give love, that's all.

Mind: For me, this is easy too. I want peace of mind.

Soul: Okay. I can help you to do these things easily.

Mind: Really?

Heart: How?

Soul: Well, for a start, you just need to get rid of your ego (the little 'i'). Then, once you have mastered this, destroy, and remove your desire (which is the want) and that's it. You'll always be left with what you really need ... which is peace and love.

Mind: I seem to remember learning that many lifetimes ago!

Heart: Well, thank you Mind. How come you couldn't remind me of this.

Mind: I don't know ... the truth seemed to get buried in all that false stuff. Anyway, Heart, perhaps if you were more open, you'd have felt the answer long ago, too.

Heart: That's true. In a way, I so longed to be loved. I have even forgotten to share my own, as I didn't want to get hurt, becoming bruised by all that's around me.

Soul: I am so pleased you two are talking properly once again. Do you know this might just work out?

Mind: Eh?

Soul: Well, I think we secretly all wish for the same thing!

Heart: We do?

Soul: Yes, the truth.

Mind: Sure, I can go along with that, because I feel that I have been searching for the answers way before I can even remember!

Heart: So, do you know the secret then?

Mind: What secret?

Heart: Oh, I don't mean of what the secret is, but what the secret does.

Mind: I'm confused now.

Soul: Hang on Heart. Why complicate matters, like you often do?

Heart: Sorry.

Soul: That's alright. Hey, listen up, as it's really simple—it's just that you should know 'thyself'.

Mind: Oh.

Heart: Yes, I believe I have heard this before … thousands of years ago!

Soul: Yes. By knowing who and what you are, then you can 'become'.

Mind: Really? Become what?

Soul: The truth.

Heart: That's it, yes, I remember! When you realise and know that you are part of creation and pure love, then you'll understand everything.

Mind: Ah ha … I see now. I am I!

Soul: Eureka!

Heart: How wonderful!

Soul: Don't you see? You, living as the Heart, need love to function, because if you didn't, you would just shrivel up and die.

Heart: That's true.

I AM I The Indweller of Your Heart—Book Three

Soul: You, living as the Mind, need love to radiate from the Heart so that you can elevate those pure thoughts.

Mind: Right! Hence, when those good thoughts come back to me, they'll flow back to the heart too, where they can continue to grow and bloom.

Soul: Yes indeed. Then the sweet fragrance will illuminate me so that I can shine for others to see.

Mind and Heart: Wow, so we are all connected after all!

Soul: Of course, we always were. But Mind, you had forgotten us and Heart, well ... you felt all alone, didn't you, which just kept the door shut so that you couldn't feel our presence.

Heart: I'm sorry. I hadn't meant to. Please, both forgive me; I will always be open now, I promise.

Mind: Me too. I'll try to stop negativity from reaching you and will always do my very best to let no one sense or feel it.

Soul: I feel very proud of you both, as I know that life for the 'body', which does its best to look after us, can only get better now.

Mind: Yes, let's not try to stress it anymore.

Heart: Agreed. If I am happy, then it will be happy too.

Mind: Absolutely. I am not going to give in to false desires anymore; you know.

Soul: That's great to hear!

Heart: And the other thing, let's not be so distant with each other in the future.

Mind: Sure thing. After all, we are 'one' aren't we!

Soul: Hallelujah. Let's give the body some rest now, shall we?

Heart: Yes, some pause for thought for the Mind.

Mind: Great, such reflection is good for the Soul.

Soul: Indeed, that is so. It brings love to the heart too, in which we can all enjoy.

Heart/Mind/Soul: Amen to that!

LESSON 22:
WHISPERS

I see each and every one of you all the time. Therefore, no matter where, when, or how you perceive me, I am with—and within thee—twenty-four hours a day and seven days a week. Can you still believe this ... after all that you have experienced, said, or done?

Because of the way you live, your busy lives are often being led by either your hidden (or even displayed) desires, both to achieve and/or 'accumulate' within the impermanent world. As such, I ask whether you can still see, sense, or hear me? Is love and truth at the forefront of your mind? Or is the light inside your heart pushed to one side due to frustration, ego, or even pride?

Upon your continuing journey within your current embodiment, is your motivation still intact? Do you have the drive to achieve your goal of self-realization, peace, and bliss? Are the earthbound pressures of work, family concerns, money, or even one's health really intervene, trying to force a wedge and keep us apart in some way, shape, or form? Or, has your belief and faith in our 'one-ness' been as strong, or become even stronger than ever before?

Well, know that each soul can only answer these questions for themselves. And through the connection of the heart, I can be as involved or as distant as you wish or intend me to be. I can be your friend, confidant, guide, and strength, or am merely just a name both cast and whispered upon the wind, which fades away like an echo.

Therefore, when you keep focused on your purpose, the existence of our unity will not be a snapshot of what might or could have been. Unlike an old photograph, buried deep within the album of so-called treasured moments, you must remember that you have 'captured' me. Inside then, the soul can bloom with the fragrance of love. And even though your body changes every day, I am the constant, the reminder, and the true picture which you can continue to develop in truth.

Realise too, the light which is both within and without—and in all things—is both positive and negative in its simplest form. You might say that the darkroom is a mysterious place, or is it just those feelings which can only be created, expanded, and exposed by your very own thoughts. These highlight and develop one's own innate fears or concerns from the current, or even previous embodiment's, through karma.

As a result, by re-creating your thoughts ... new words and deeds can transform the way you live, work, rest, and play. What they then reveal for others to see, and experience is the joy, peace, and happiness which flows from you. Without even thinking, your smile and tone of voice and your body language all help you shine more brightly for others to sense, which uplifts their own thoughts and demeanour.

Unlike the modern age in which you currently live, no technology or digital makeover is required. You should never feel you have blemishes or facets that you need to disguise or hide. You are what you are. In whose 'eye's' does someone think they need to be perfect on the outside, anyway? Human nature picks or finds fault no matter whether you are a King, Queen, a president, or even if you walk the streets with nothing but the clothes upon your back.

No matter what the exterior garment reveals, it is with the inner 'I' which illuminates and transcends. It is your character and personality—and above all, your heart—rather than the bodily appearance and image that's portrayed ... which then shines through what you say or do.

One can create as many illusions as one wishes to make. You can even try (if you like) to deceive yourself from being who or what you are. But light sees all as an eternal witness to truth. This is why one might deny others of the true you, but not me.

As I have always stated, there are no secrets that one can keep, so I hope this reminder does not perturb anyone or anything. Only anxiety or dread of something—or someone—can ever cause that. So, like I have always said, do not fear when I am near.

You do not need to shout, remonstrate, or scream to make yourself heard. Words are secondary to communicate love. Take two lovers; one does not need to speak to the other to understand their feelings and inner connection. Likewise, it is your heart which whispers to me when you are happy and glad or are in despair and sad. Each resonates and communicates as energy to, from, and through me, as we are 'one'.

Your emotions can all be subtle and kind, or they can pierce the ether through time and dimension like arrows, sometimes missing their intended 'targets' whereby they inflict pain and anguish on those who step into the firing line, either intentionally—to protect and/or as a sacrifice—to aid another soul. You could class such acts as fate, divine providence, or karmic balancing, but truth is in the 'I' of the beholder, remember?

So, what can, or will you say or send out today? By connecting with your heart, you'll need to listen out for the soft voice of truth. Once recognized and understood, you can continue to shine and, therefore, link, causing stronger bonds and ties.

In your daily dealings with family, friends, or work colleagues, try to reduce those raised voices or tones as they only strain these threads, cords or chains which connect you all. They become more like 'Chinese' whispers, which distort the true meaning of your intentions and wishes. Ultimately, don't you just wish the best for yourself? If so, then you only need to want the same for others, too.

Please understand right now, you do not need to be loud to be larger than life. You can communicate softly, sweetly, and even in whispers, so each moment of every day can be the new beginning of your continued journey. Eventually, all will come to understand that you, the aspirant, the devotee, the pilgrim, or a disciple of truth, have only ever travelled from 'himself' to 'himself'. Shh … it's not a secret. You just need to remember. Amen.

LESSON 23:
STRUCTURE

There will always be a time when you can reflect upon your life, of how you currently feel, and where your destiny lies. And, if you were now gazing into the pool of love—which floats within your own heart and soul—what images do you think can be seen? Would you believe you are now a witness to the truth?

Please understand though, whenever someone goes through uncertain times, be it with work, family, or issues regarding 'home' life, they should not dwell upon or contemplate the things which they cannot control. It is better to be true to yourself and continue to rise every day with hope, optimism, and, if you can, be content.

Sometimes this can be very difficult within the world's modern structure, especially as a constant demand upon the sense's streams outward from television, radio, and so many other devices. All of them try to show that materialism is vital to your well-being, with those 'must-haves' to make you feel fulfilled.

Likewise, body image, which leads people to feel self-conscious about their appearance, and even fashion, where one is made to feel 'outdated' through commercialism and peer pressure—which is so prevalent in so many walks of life—can trick their way into your mind. It attempts to make you feel negatively about yourself in so many ways.

So, how can you maintain the status quo, and yet continue to be true to self? Well foremost, because you now understand all things are from, through and to love, it is essential that everything is seen in the same way … with both truth and light. Even though billions of people may be at different levels of experience and knowledge, please appreciate having embarked upon the same journey, in which all should nullify ego and sanctify the goal in each.

One's life can draw parallels to how a house is built. Without strong foundations, the home can succumb to the turbulence of exterior events. Wind, fire, or water can bring it crumbling down. Likewise, without strength from family connections—which include togetherness, support, and encouragement of a father, mother, brother, or sister—a home becomes cold, uninviting, and the door unwelcoming to friends and strangers alike. A household such as this can quickly swallow up goodwill and faith. Like quicksand, it removes all traces of one's previous struggle to avoid its vice like grip.

True strength remains hidden, like underpinning, which carries the weight of wood, brick, or stone. So too with love, for it bears those burdens of your very own karmic debt. However, the walls of faith can rise once more, and, when built with trust, they become even stronger. Know that it acts just like mortar; interlacing to form an impregnable barrier, keeping our exterior negativity, trouble, and strife. They can give you hope to overcome such things because you'll realise that the real enemy comes from your very own doubt and despair.

Now imagine the roof of the home. Just like any structure, it needs to be connected properly, fixed firmly in position for it to function as it should. No matter if it's made of wood, straw, metal, or slate. If misaligned, it will fail, letting in both wind and rain.

It is the same for the mind; and the mental aspects of your 'being'. If one's aspirations become aloof or detached from reality—becoming disturbed and going wayward through fear, anxiety, or pain—then it cannot function correctly, either. One's thoughts will fly upon both wind and ether, causing not only havoc where they fall, but they will return to the source … which only agitates and increases the uncertainty, anguish, and misery.

It is the mind which can therefore inflict more damage than anything else. This is where weaknesses will firstly be felt, with all sorts and manners of illusion attempting to take hold, trying to dismantle those very walls of strength. Lack of self-esteem, desperation, and depression are just a few of the conditions which fight like inner demons. They try to overthrow and unbalance righteousness, love, and peace.

You should now realise we are connected and interlinked much more like a home; with the body of 'man' and me as one. Through understanding and belief, no single part fails but will hold true. Know then, like a strong roof, which accepts and sheds the falling rain, so too the mind can dissipate falling tears just as easily … but only once self-realization is gained in truth.

This will enable you to carry each other through those so-called good and bad times. And, over the greatest fear of all, death. Once this knowledge and wisdom is held deep within the heart, you will see the Sun (Son) has not disappeared but re-emerges from behind the clouds of illusion. Like sunlight, positive energy will shine down upon each one of you for your continued growth and strength.

Hence, in life, do not feel you are just striving towards a destination. One's destiny and journey has no 'ending'. It is not like coming back from a holiday, returning to the house built beside the roadside. The current rebirth to the physical is for a purpose and a reason, but it is not the 'be all and end all'.

When the time is right, every soul will depart their temporary home upon the 'earth-plane'. They will take flight and soar into peace and bliss, and within a higher plane and frequency of energy and power. Remember too, beyond the beyond is no fantasy. It is a fact and a true reality … for my heart and home are where you truly belong. Its structure of love and light is eternal, and you are already within it, but you just need to know, feel, and believe it to be true. Amen.

LESSON 24:
LIFE—PATH

As you start to write this message, you are uncertain of what it will contain, and of the why and the how it will teach and guide you. This is okay, for sometimes it is good not to know or have any inkling, like a mystery to be unravelled—then shared—with anticipation and eagerness.

Life can be like this too. You believe you understand where you're headed, only to discover or find yourself in another time, place, or going in another direction. Perhaps to explore and enjoy a new adventure?

Can you then—even if you are in middle or old age—ever feel this way again? Could the journey enthral you as much as the journey's end, which entices you with so much potential and promise? Or does one's own thoughts of uncertainty, anguish, or fear bring about palpitations, breathless sighs, and a longing for the answers of both heart and mind?

Time and time again, I say that if you can trust in yourself—and therefore in me—everything you do and everywhere you go in the physical world will be precisely when you are meant to. The same cannot be said of (and for) your soul. You cannot arrive, or believe you are going somewhere like a heaven, as by now—through self-realization—you'll understand you will have simply come full circle.

In contrast with your daily lives, I see the rush, hustle, and bustle of one's work, rest, and play. Places to be, people to see, work, or things to do. Breakneck speed to 'exist' may be considered multi-tasking, motivational, or inspiring to some, but in reality, it is no way to live.

One could simplify such things. Try viewing the countryside whilst sitting upon a bullet train compared with looking at it while on a double–decker bus … or even compare a supersonic aircraft to a jumbo jet. The former undoubtedly will arrive and travel from A to B more quickly. The latter gives the opportunity to view, pause, reflect, and to contemplate during the process. In life, whose deadlines are you trying to meet? In relation to one's tasks, who are you attempting to please?

If all people are sparks of divinity, then each is 'Godly'. Therefore, in service to each other, those fruits of your labour—which we have discussed before—are secondary and inconsequential. Once again, I ask whether you trust in me? And do you believe I can take care of all your needs? If so, then there is no call for worry and to fret. All will materialize as and when it should, and not sooner or later than this.

I understand that for many, it is the letting go of those make believe 'reins' ... and accepting the unknown which can be difficult to achieve. However, this is so important to grasp. If every thought, word, or deed is deemed to originate from, through, and by you—the imagined 'do-er'—then all this shows is that you feel separate from me. How can this ever be the case when we are 'one'?

Remember, I know you better than you can ever know yourself, because the bond and chains of love eternally link your soul to me. Hence, the records of who, what, and also where you have ever been (and everything in between) are available to me as the witness to truth.

Unlike a 'black-box' within an aircraft, which can become detached, its information and history lost or destroyed—for example, through fire or water—no such occurrence can ever take place with your heart and soul. Everything man made is impermanent, but divinity is everlasting. It cannot be misread or misinterpreted in the light's permanence.

Repeatedly, through the course of these books, I have reiterated the only decision you need to make is what to do with the time that has been pre-sent to you. One does not have to be religious or even follow a faith to 'shine'. Your attitudes and thoughts during simple everyday tasks and occurrences highlight and indicate your current well-being, demeanour, and happiness.

For example, do you feel annoyed or angry when it rains, and you're soaked to the skin? Or do you feel blessed to feel it upon your face, knowing it provides for both nature and man alike? Do you become frustrated by the delays on the road or are you grateful it isn't you or a family member caught up in a so-called 'accident', suffering from physical or emotional pain?

Likewise, are you humbled and feeling blessed when a stranger offers you their seat, a drink or something to eat ... or do you become apprehensive and fearful of a possible ulterior motive? Are you proud and glad to be who you are, or do you feel the cards were not handed out correctly, being stacked against you from the very start?

Do not believe in bad luck either. Everything is cause and effect. Karma and balance rests upon the individual scales of justice that each soul carries. Indeed, you 'weigh' in both light and dark, and the positive and negative, with every beat of your heart. You cannot deny or cheat oneself—or any other soul—for, unlike a marketplace, one cannot barter for goods or sell what you feel you do not need (or no longer belong) in your life.

Each day that you arise is an opportunity to gain and share knowledge and wisdom through one's experiences. If you can simply be glad and not sad, you understand that the peaks and troughs, those ups and downs upon your road ahead, can be enjoyed. Why should you fear the horizon when I am within, beside, above, and below you?

Please try to take pleasure in whatever you do. Or at least what the mind or heart becomes engaged in—this way you can give the best of yourself, and the goodness will reflect on others at the same time. If something is worth doing, then do it well. Doesn't this age-old expression still ring true?

Of course, these are all your very own choices and decisions. You can walk free from the bondage and shadows you and others may have cast to step forward into the light. It is here and here alone that can fulfil your true potential upon this life-path of truth. Why not live it, breathe it, and become who you were re-born to be? Amen.

LESSON 25:
LAZY DAYS?

You sit and write upon the warmest evening of the year so far, and all around you, one can hear the 'buzz' of life. From beautiful birdsong and with the hum of bees and wasps to the occasional fly, all of creation is blossoming.

Finally, after many weeks of rain and those cloudy days and nights, summer has truly arrived. Across the valley, the Sun's haze dwindles, leaving a picturesque scene of green and golden fields. The hedgerows and trees, which are now in full leaf, frame the 'image' in all its splendour. And, yes indeed, nature is at its finest. An artist's pallet would do well to emulate and capture this for another's eyes to behold.

As so often the case, one will survey such surroundings, yet actually forget to stop and listen to the world about you. However, by making the time to be still and contemplate on such serenity and peace, you will feel recharged and also quite content too.

It is—in fact—very easy to take life for granted when rushing through the day. However, when it is possible to place the mind and body from fast forward onto pause, you will realise just how much you're actually missing. Be it the radiant flowers in the borders, blossom in the hedgerows, birds upon the wing, a spider in its web, the ladybird on a leaf, and wood lice making their merry way across the soil and wood … these are all but a glimpse of the oneness of life.

Now, within this moment, the warm air is like a blessing bestowed. I sense and feel much gratitude from many hearts as it uplifts the mind and brings well-being. As you look upwards, the swifts and swallows both sweep and glide, bringing elegance to the sky above. You pause and reflect once again. Your appreciation towards me beams both inside and out … and in turn, I place my loving grace over thee. The well of thy heart is full to the brim at times like these, so enjoy the happiness you feel and also send it back into the ether.

A slight breeze descends, weaving through the leaves and branches—but this is only my breath and sigh of joy, which envelops everything—as they seemingly wave to each one of you. Whether you sense and believe this, and know me upon this 'level', it is only for the individual to say, but within the soul you all understand me. Realise that it is acknowledging me in all things, which helps to pose the questions which must be answered in and through you with love, light, and truth.

I understand when I witness your life becoming so hectic—from family, work, or home issues—one may often wish for a long lazy day in the Sun. Although I stated earlier about 'recharging the batteries,' know it is not so much a physical rest that many require, but often the time one needs to take to ease the restless mind. This brings balance. It also provides a constant repetitive boost to one's health and happiness, no matter what the weather outside your door.

Remember, meditation is no more than becoming detached from desire in its various ways, shapes, and forms. Indeed, worldly attachment can blur your thought processes, influencing your actions and ultimately leading to confusion and illusion. It can affect you emotionally and spiritually, which is like trying to look at the midday Sun, making your eyes squint and stream with tears of discontent. So, why would you do this—even briefly—when its power can cause blindness? And this is exactly the same in terms of being kept in the dark by enveloping your 'all' within the impermanent world.

Frequently, I have explained you should ideally 'live' in the world but not be part of it. By 'living', I mean being kind, supportive, understanding, peaceful, truthful, non-violent, and acting with and from love. You can do all of these things, yet still recognize that the material world is transient. It is an experience for both heart and soul on many levels. Ultimately, it is part of the education you require, or else you would not have been re-born to the physical plane.

Coming off this cycle of rebirth and death (through your own self-realization) is the most important aspect of your path and journey. As this is so, your love can blossom beyond imagination with a sweet fragrance. And just like a flower's, I can carry it upon my breath beyond time, space, and all dimensions.

Now, as you sit, the Sun dips below the horizon. Even as it does so, the air remains warm to the skin. A wonderful feeling, without doubt. You can still make out the buttercups and daisies growing up from the grass, and these remind you of such beauty in all forms.

It's a little darker now. Two bats suddenly swoop into view. Circling repeatedly overhead, they feast upon the insects. Of course, they cannot see them, but use their radar and echo to know precisely where they are, just like an inner awareness. In comparison, most of you have all your senses, but how many use the internal link—like a sixth sense—to find and witness the truth? Can you, or do you, even want to?

Looking about you, shadows which were earlier cast from the burning

Sun have since blended and faded away. Similarly, those shadows cast by your own karma must now begin to disappear. For far too long they lie stretched behind you, like a black silhouette reaching into the distance. And like a heavy burden, you have dragged this weight off—and form—previous incarnations around with you.

However, you are more than ready to offload such things now, through the power of love and truth. Gradually, by continuing to walk in the light, the shadow and gloom will become closer and closer to you as the Sun will rise once more to shine high above you. There will then be a point at which the karmic debt and darkness will be erased. The Sun and divine light will fall behind you instead, to lead and gently guide you forward to the eternal glory in me.

Then, you will have earned for yourself a true lazy day, where you can bask amongst family, friends, and pets. Their love and energy will make you realise beyond all doubt that love knows no bounds. It is here, there, and everywhere ... being always and forever into eternity. Amen.

LESSON 26:
UNKNOWN

Welcome to one and all, upon another glorious sunny evening. Once again, when you can find—or rather make—the time to be still, you will feel the serenity both within and out. And, not only will you find me (the inner voice), but you'll also understand so much more. It is here and here alone one can make the unknown ... known.

Since time immemorial, humanity has always sought the answers to three typical questions. Are there other intelligent life forms—or beings—out there? Is there life after death? And is there a God? The answer to each is yes, of course there is! All three questions are actually linked. Each one implies a division when there is none. How can the heart, mind, and soul be separate ... when they form the whole, each influencing and affecting each other?

Similarly, countless beings upon different worlds (and within many dimensions) have reached various levels of understanding. Some less, but some far greater in terms of both technology and wisdom, than planet Earth. This does not make you—or them—more worthy of my love ... but I hope this will encourage you to search inside yourself. This will enable and help you know the without ... or so-called 'out there'.

When people think of alien life, they may assume it must be like watching a Hollywood sci-fi movie. But intelligent life exists a heartbeat or only a thought away. All life is energy. Hence, a 'body's' vibration rate or frequency is just different from your own, that is all.

It could be relatively easy then to imagine the physicality of a creature or a being upon a different planet, but less so to comprehend such life elsewhere. Who actually states something has to breathe oxygen, require water, or need any physical sustenance to survive or thrive? Life is as diverse and obscure only as far as you set those limitations within your heart and mind.

Know, too, that millions of souls, creatures, and beings walk upon the Earth—both by night and by day—but remain on alternative frequencies. Their energy seemingly obscured from all the senses. However, because we are 'one', you only need to re-tune yourself—like a radio—to another channel or station, to hear, see, feel, and comprehend other forms of 'life'.

This information may, of course, seem common knowledge to some. But again, only simplicity is required. People just need to tune to the so-called 'medium' wave to receive what they—or others—need to know at whatever level they think or believe they are at.

I witness too that nearly every 'birth' onto the physical plane can give rise to a fear of death. Some will always state that once you die, that is it. No amount of explanation or evidence can change their viewpoint or belief. Right until the very moment before their passing, the unknown may haunt them ... like a mysterious figure at the window, or the shadow which lurks and creeps within the dark recesses of their mind. Remember, death is only a veil which hides the truth of everlasting life for every soul.

Regarding me—I am I/God—it is easier to doubt than to believe, is it not? For many, though, the inner connection is more than enough. Whereas others, because of their fear (or denial) of their own experiences, may somehow appear to take them even further away from me.

Imagine if you can, two couples ... both fathers and mothers, whose children have been murdered. On one side, there can be anger, hatred, confusion, despair, and pain, becoming so unbearable their hearts feel ripped in two. On the other, their pain may just be as deep. But through an internal understanding—which one may call faith, a belief, or even wisdom—they can forgive ... but they do not (and never will) forget.

This will help and enable them to continue to live and grow within the knowledge that love always prevails. In contrast, the inability to transcend and 'move on' will forever be like a nerve ending, which induces both sporadic and repeatable anguish. This is an emotional torture that threatens the well-being of the body, heart, and soul.

Of course, people often shout, scream, and raise their fist in anger ... as if I am up above—sitting upon a throne—casting out favour and goodwill on some, and misery and despair upon others. "There can't be a God if he/she can let this happen!" Then, on the other side of the coin, there can be elation and tears of joy when one's hopes and dreams become fulfilled. I then hear and feel, "Thank you dear God, for your grace and mercy."

Please realise that I am not your scales of justice, but as I recently stated, love knows no bounds. That said, so can darkness, decay and fear. With every positive, there will be a negative. For every up, there is a down. There is always an opposite.

Comprehend that your thoughts can bring about change, both within and also out. They can also create, or they can destroy. So, in every life, there will be a moment where you will need to decide what side of the fence you're currently at or will endeavour to be on.

This isn't my judgment, but is just a fact that each of you has 'created' through your own thoughts, words, and deeds. Life may indeed try to induce you to disbelieve and distrust the unknown. But, by embracing the challenge to know thyself through love, truth, kindness, and peace ... your soul can relearn all that can ever be known. Amen.

LESSON 27:
CONTINUITY

In this age (especially now), most of you long for a sense of stability, a period where life can seem to bring a normality to everyday living. Yet with an ever-changing world which is becoming so fast-paced—and with new technology demanding one's attention almost twenty-four hours a day—what can you cling to? Where can one find a sense of belonging ... which is purposeful, forthright, reserved, and a role-model for the many?

One may instinctively think of someone in a sacred place; a religious figurehead, maybe a guru, or perhaps even a famous 'celebrity'. But in fact, a shining example of a dignified soul, who encourages and desires happiness for all, is none other than Queen Elizabeth II.

She currently celebrates her Diamond Jubilee year, commemorating 60 years as monarch. This is a significant 'time' period that you associate with having 'passed' by. Her reign has given a structure. Just like a framework, it aids and guides the people, who are no longer being deemed as merely 'subjects' to be controlled by anger, fear ... or threatened like those of bygone eras.

Through democracy, there has been a balance in which love for the country and its population has endured. It levels the peaks and troughs of, and through, experience. Therefore, she is admired and respected and remains forever popular during political and economic changes or turmoil.

From her early years, came the responsibility to uphold both moral and ethical values, remaining dignified and honourable, even when scandals and disruptive 'forces' encircled the monarchy like vultures looking for fallen prey. One could say, of course, that she has been well advised or even directed by knowledgeable staff. Ultimately, just like within each of your lives, all thoughts, words, and deeds come down to one's personal choice and, you could say, your 'free-will'.

As nothing stands still in life, be it with family, friends, work, and even the world and everything upon it; this change is the one constant that is ever present. So, by living with those true human values that we have spoken about before, you become adaptable and flexible. All the while, you must realise you are an important cog within the wheel and cycle of humanity ... which indeed you all are.

As explained before, you do not need to question yourself, asking whether you are big or small within the grand scheme of things. All souls are eternal, and their value limitless. Only upon the 'earth-plane' can ego manifest and attempt to dictate that someone is better, or deemed of greater importance, than another.

So then, Queen Elizabeth II is such a wonderful case in point because she displays true inner qualities. Yet all beings contain the same, though they often choose not to convey them. Likewise, many feel that they are so low—as if at the bottom of the ladder or some sort of 'pecking' order—which unfortunately devalues themselves and their own time. Please try to understand, each and every one of you does not need 'Royal' blood running through your veins to show your true worth, because you are all the descendants of truth.

Yes indeed, the direct linage is forever connected to, through, and from my heart. And the seat of your soul is my throne, which forms a part of my kingdom. Time, space, and all dimensions are but fragments of me and the power that is I. Because this is so, then you are also the same.

Know too that I have never 'ruled' like any Kings or Queens of 'old'; dispensing justice, pleasure, or pain upon a whim. Your history is full of such thoughts, words, and deeds ... which have attempted to divide and conquer rather than to provide and protect, or to lead and guide to truth. Someone must also reap all such seeds which are sown. Know that I will never chastise or criticize but remain vigilant of all things and every aspect of life.

Remember, you are glorious, a divine spark of love. One has the crown of my heart above and within your own. All known (and unknown) earthly trinkets or precious jewels cannot ever compare. If you could only look from the outside in, then these words would not be required, because recognition of such would be instantaneous.

Therefore, in those moments during your life, when everything around you is changing—whirling like an emotional tornado, ripping through hopes and dreams—it is your own self–realization which reveals the real continuity which every soul craves for. As each heart requires protection, guidance, knowledge, and wisdom, the strength and peace which brings stability is not in any sacred building, a so-called safe house or stronghold - it is within you!

This true fortitude and fortress can withstand every test because I built the foundations with love. Pillars of faith and hope support your whole being. These enable your mind to repel negative traits, discontent, and desire if you can just embrace and let them do so.

Consider now, though, one's physical home, which may be very humble.

Even a cardboard box can provide a temporary barrier to the elements. On the other side of the coin, a palace can also bring its own concerns and problems. The fear of losing privacy, or even a lapse or break of 'security'. It may have many rooms, but the body can only lay down its head and fall asleep in one, so perhaps this is a choice too far?

Please believe you are all truly within my mansion. All learn on different levels, walking through the corridors and passages of time; working and living in halls of knowledge, experience, and wisdom - eternally wishing to escape from the revolving door and cycle or birth and death. And understand this: while you are re-educating yourselves, you remember bits and pieces of your own reality both here and there. This is the whom, what, why, and the wherefores of life and your existence … and how you are all connected and linked in an unbreakable chain of light.

So, while you go about your daily tasks and your work, rest, and play, perhaps you could consider where real duty lies. Is it toward the Queen, a King, or a country? What about your employer? Your friends or family? Without disrespect or to belittle any so-called 'authority' upon the 'earth-plane', appreciate that it is foremost to (and for) you and your own heart and soul.

Why? Well, everything stems from 'self'. It is perpetual. If every person was aware of this, then love and light would instantly eradicate anger, hate, deceit, and fear. Hands would join; held across the world to unite humanity in truth. Hearts would heal, souls cleansed, and legacies fulfilled. A real reign of peace would envelope all lands, while every and continent could raise a Universal flag to signal the end of uncertainty, trepidation, and all confusion and illusion.

Therein lies the continuity that is inherent in all of creation. I have eternally given this within—and upon—every creature, being, heart and soul and all life … forever and a day. Amen.

LESSON 28:

HOLLOW

Many people continue to yearn and search from outside of themselves. They look towards the exterior world for illumination and meaning, but there will forever be the feeling that something is missing ... like an incomplete jigsaw puzzle.

One may notice such because the picture or scene has a space ... or in the case of one's life, you become unfulfilled, with hopes and dreams falling by the wayside with disappointment or regret. If you currently find yourself, or seem to approach this scenario—no matter what your age, colour, or sex—would you just accept it as 'fate'? Or could you pick yourself up from the floor once more?

What experience of your body, mind, or soul could help you re-ignite the passion of, and for, the truth? How about gazing upon a beautiful sunrise or sunset, or reading or listening to sacred words or poems? Perhaps you can find this spark within a warm smile, or feeling a loving embrace which somehow keeps the flame of love and light ... alight? One only needs to pause and reflect upon the 'wonder' all around you to feel amazed at such peace and beauty. You can find this in colour, texture, shapes, or sounds, which transcends to touch your heart and soul.

If this wasn't the case, perhaps there are those who would call such an individual blind, morbid, depressed ... or worse still, heartless, soul-less, or even hollow. Understand, though, no one would really wish to be viewed or be known this way. In truth, any creature or person (and soul) would resemble a zombie. Others might state they resemble the 'living dead', but in fact, they are neither 'living' nor 'dead', in the true sense of these words.

So, as you make your way through life, are you on 'auto-pilot'? If so, do you really believe that you can live in a vacuum, devoid of truth, love, and happiness? In reality, would such a vacuum exist 'inside' or 'outside' of you? Sadly, in continually blaming oneself, you can get caught in a downward spiral. A forceful sense of desire, fear, hate, or anguish can seem to suck the very life force and energy—the positive aspect of both living and being—from within you.

Every one of you must remember you can be in control of how you feel and react to any situation. By constantly monitoring your thoughts, you can change so much emotionally, physically, mentally, and spiritually, both inside and out. You can, therefore, attract positive energy, goodwill, kindness, generosity, and peace into your life and to the door of your home.

That said, in today's society, one might imagine that they would have to go somewhere to create, change, or even repair some aspect within themselves. But what could need fixing? Does someone need to change their opinions, beliefs, attitudes, or even their looks and appearance to satisfy another? And, with your opinions, feelings, thoughts, hopes, and dreams, can there really be a so-called 'empty' space after all?

Instead, by removing any rose-coloured glasses, you can see with the internal lens of your heart ... which will allow you to witness the truth. You'll know that you are not merely this body, but a soul residing in a 'vessel'. This enables you to remain in this lower, denser vibration and energy to relearn and grow. So, when karma has been fulfilled and your life 'complete'—be it for only one second or minute, one hour or day, one month or year, or even three scores and ten—the soul then departs, and the vessel becomes lifeless to the naked eye.

People will often assume their loved one is still in their arms. They associate memories of their presence with the physical body, but they are now hollow in the true sense of the word. For all this, they are even closer to them than can be imagined. The veil—this curtain of deceit called 'death'—is only an illusion, like a mirage. Some may feel confused by this, implying I even contradict words or meanings. I urge you to feel them inside of you ... and not with the mind.

One's body, becoming 'hollow' through death (and not through a way of living) can be reinterpreted as being 'holy' or whole. Though—while in your embodiment—it is unfortunately easier to believe in separateness and division, both from each other and me. With your self-realization, all becomes clear. Selfishness leads to selflessness. Hate turns to love. And through your divine spark, you witness every soul just as holy and sacred as you all are to me.

So, rather than an emptiness, where one lives each day seemingly without purpose, I can fulfil you. You will feel it and know the difference inside and out of your being. Your words, thoughts, and deeds, which were once diverse, and now seemingly 'pigeon-holed' into various components of life —like work, rest, and play and full of desires to please the mind—will change.

Subtly at first, but over time, you will become cognizant of what you're actually thinking. The consequences of such, and what you speak and do, will be kinder and of a more caring nature. These will then flourish, allowing you to nurture relationships with friends, family, kith, and kin in ways of truth. And not from what one can gain, accumulate, or even seek for 'self'.

This pretend 'void' is nothing other than the illusion of doubt which attempts to eat away from within. Left unchecked, it can easily change from nagging doubts or frustrations which lead to anger or hate. Before you know it, they push the goodness and love to one side. It might seem much simpler to forget you ever had it at all, but you have love, are love, and always will be.

Therefore, I ask you to rely on and trust in yourself … and therefore me. As we are 'one' body, one light, one truth, then you only need to believe. You can do this; you only need to try. Once you do, it is self-perpetuating, because, like a thirst, it will need to be quenched.

Indeed, 'truth' can be searched for in faraway places, upon sacred sites and from many people … whether they are paupers, presidents, or kings. However, it is in your heart that you will find your true self and me and the truth which is right for your soul. This way, what is usually seen by others (your exterior self, the wrapper and shell), will be replaced by the beautiful radiance and glow of your true essence … the inside 'out'.

The shining light—which is your reality—will enrich others through your gentle touch, soothing words, and kind gestures. This may surprise those who know you, and more so … those you don't. in fact, even those strangers who pass through your day and life seemingly unnoticed.

Know that change in any way does not need or have to wait for tomorrow. By truly living for today, tomorrow will take care of itself. This way, the daily seeds you sow will grow and come to bear the fruit of truth with true human kindness. Amen.

LESSON 29:
SLAVE

Your heart hears my call once more. One often imagines it to be no more than a whisper in the wind. This frequently falls upon the deaf ears of so many—throughout time, space, and all dimensions. It is important to know then that I feel you always, in all ways. Know that all your worries, concerns, wishes, hopes, and dreams echo and reverberate like silent screams, both through and to me.

Indeed, numerous souls believe this so-called 'time'—between listening out for me—may repeatedly seem as if an eternity has passed. In reality, it is only the blink of an eye, or a snap of your fingers to me. And because you now sense my presence—instead of the rush, anguish, and sheer pace of life—tears fall from the well of your heart. This proves the peace, tranquillity, and the one-ness of being that you feel is real.

You cannot miss me, only your senses try to dictate that you do. Having previously mentioned, by removing those rose-coloured spectacles, you become a witness to the truth. Within silence (the Sai-Lens), any pretence of separation and division falls away ... like shadows removed by the light of the Sun (and Son).

Therefore, if you can now focus upon the title of this lesson, you will still wish to consider two clear aspects (from your thoughts) it conjures up. But unlike a magician, who only reveals what he or she wants you to see or believe, you will understand there is no sleight of hand, or disguising words or tricks here.

First, your mind may think of a master and servant scenario. It realises deep inside there is only one master worthy of that name. Also, regarding those concerned, a slave could be seen as worthless, unintelligent, dirty, without purpose ... and treated accordingly. However, like a mirror, this is only a reflection of their so-called 'master' ... who believes they are in control of the person, animal, or being, by their own thoughts, words, and deeds.

Attitudes and practices of such have never had any place at all within society. Now, especially within this new age of democracy and peace, the truth needs to envelope all human beings. It is demeaning on so many levels of life and consciousness. Not only to those who try to impose their will, and but for those who are manipulated, cajoled, or forced to accept or comply to another's ideals or way of existence.

Second, please understand that each person who has been re-born onto the 'earth-plane' is actually under your own inner threat and danger of becoming a slave. Not to me, or even to another person or being, but to oneself ... trapped by your very own senses. This is because such traits as jealousy, desire, and ego all influence and constantly become magnets for the mind, attracting dissatisfaction, discontent, and a lack of morality towards others and, worst of all, for and to yourself.

Again, particularly in these current times, be it through peer pressure, control from the television (tell-lie-vision), or by any form of 'media'—as well as by 'governing' bodies or associations—you can be carried along as if on a conveyor belt. This appears to give no choice or even allow you to pause for breath, and so you become unable to take stock of your current situation.

As a result, it becomes apparent that only through one's trials and tribulations do you reconsider what you are doing, where you are going, or how you are living as a person and soul. Instead of believing that these times are detrimental to your own (or your families') wellbeing and future, they can become accepted as an alternative, as real periods when you can grow stronger, both mentally and spiritually.

If you were to ask anyone who has had a lifesaving operation, been rescued from a perilous situation, emerged from the depths of depression, or even overcome the dependence from any physical habit, then not only are the circumstances surrounding such now seen with a fresh perspective ... but their reason and purpose of life—and living—becomes much more focused. Simply put, many could surely state an illness or any 'loss' helps them to focus on the quality of their own time. Undeniably, it provides a new and different viewpoint. In fact, they often explain that they now realise, wish, feel, and need to live for 'today'.

Appreciate negative energy, both dissolve and dissipate. Positive energy ushers in a new beginning—a new dawn of hope—with anticipation and gladness. Like a chain reaction, enthusiasm then spreads to others. In turn, larger networks of love and light radiate both far and wide, and all these can stem from a simple change of thought.

Be aware you can change. You can live and become who you were re-born to be ... by simply making small and seemingly unnoticeable changes to your attitudes, words, and deeds. Why not think about what has occurred today? Who have you spoken to? Consider what you saw, heard, tasted and touched ... and those notions and thoughts which flowed through and across your mind at the speed of light, too. Now compare them to those which have festered, dragging, and lowering your energy with annoyance, illusion, confusion, hatred, jealousy, and anger.

Do you recognize any of these? How did, or will you now, react? Any so-called mistake can be overridden and forgotten. You can re-learn what drives you, and then this can make you become the real you … and not who others may wish you to be.

Know and truly believe that you are not slaves. Not to each other and certainly not to me. You are eternally free. All forms and aspects of physical and sensory slavery within life and energy need to be eradicated. Do not justify or feel you have ever become a victim of circumstance but see every situation and scenario as the opportunity for growth, and to expand the love that you truly are.

Fully recognize slavery as ugly. It is energy in a gross and dense form, while your divine essence is more beautiful than you could ever contemplate or comprehend. Try to radiate this one reality. You can truly blossom, letting the fragrance of your love travel like seeds cast upon the wind of my breath, touching, and reaching those who need or require it. Know and trust you will shine forever. My grace is abundant, and it is always there for you.

So then, the opportunity to fulfil your potential lies within your very being. You only need to believe it to make it real. Understand too that these lessons, which you now read, are not, and never will be, new 'commandments' to adhere to. They are not enforceable. That would only make me a slave to my own truth … and make you the victim of your very own. As this is so, your 'will' is free. So are your choices in all you say, think or do - so make them always true. Amen.

LESSON 30:
FIELDS OF GOLD

As you gaze upon the hills and valleys far into the distance, the many fields below seem to interconnect with each other, just like a patchwork quilt. Now, with the sun shining overhead, the summer haze makes it difficult to determine which of them are ploughed, with those coming into harvest.

Please understand that within your life, the days, weeks, and months are very similar. You either sow or reap. You can ride upon the crest of a wave, while other times seem so much like hard work. Here, one's karma resembles clods of soil—weighing you down—as your journey continues along the treadmill of experience and knowledge.

However, know that one day you will all bear witness to the true fields of gold. These do not comprise a materialistic 'reward' or of anything else that can fuel desire and inflate the ego. Those things can lead to frustration, discontent, and even anger or fear. No, you'll pass right through them, like a field of feathers, and so you will then feel your walking (or rather floating), upon air.

As you focus your eyes once more, the hedgerows now become more prominent. They clearly define boundaries, which reflect those imaginary lines, drawn to decide what is thought of as 'yours' or of 'mine'. Most human beings have always tried to divide Mother Earth into pieces for themselves. They somehow desire to keep a control over someone, or something. Appreciate though, that her beauty and essence can never become the true property of 'man'. You are merely all custodians of such a precious jewel of life and light.

One may contemplate upon this more deeply at a later date, but for now, there is still more to be discovered and discussed. And so, as the sun dips below the treetops, the change of light enables you to see countless strands of cobwebs. They glisten majestically, having been cast across the tall grass, nettles, and brambles.

These are just a few examples of the natural world around you. Stop to pause and reflect upon it. Sometimes you just have to take control and switch the autopilot of life to 'off'. By disengaging the mind, you may bring the heart to the forefront of the 'self'. Each day will then reveal new and amazing insights to those simple and beautiful things to awaken your senses.

This will help all to be grateful for the brilliance of creation ... and this includes yourself!

When you can be 'still', to truly listen and feel with your heart, you remember you are not separate from any vista which captures your thoughts or imagination. Be it a mountain range, sunrise or sunset, a rainbow, or the stars glistening brightly within a summer night sky. Appreciate the spark and divine essence, and the glory of love and 'I', which connects you all.

Also, if viewed from space, Mother Earth seems to standalone in all its brilliance. And yet, if you can consider the bigger picture, there are countless 'heavenly' bodies that support and nurture nature. Only the mind attempts to restrict the possibility and plausibility of such, but like those silky threads, 'life' connects across time, space, and dimension with ease and purpose.

Hence, the Earth is like a pearl within the ocean of my love. One may even think it seems lost within the galaxies, and what man constantly describes as the Universe. Know that its nations and continents are each connected by land, sea, and even technology, but most importantly, it connects with your hearts. So, please try to not become weighed down ... by conflicts, war, anger, or fear across the world.

Be aware of the 'space' within space. Go beyond the more complex scenario (to man, that is) of matter, anti-matter, gravity, and the like. These just resemble those hedgerows between the fields upon Earth as they link and form and stabilize and enable life to exist in the ways they do. Within each are the means by which I help sustain and maintain equilibrium ... and those ideal conditions for everything to experience and grow.

I realise people will always wish to know answers to the how, why, and when, but more often than not it's only by turning back to basics one then appreciates that simplicity is the key to true knowledge and wisdom. Love is everything. Everything is love. Love is all there is.

What I mean is, without it (which is your true self), life would just crumble. It would turn to ash, then dissipate ... and disappear in all but the sense of the word. So, it is the very fabric you and I are made of. One may think of it as energy. Pure and just, unconditional, and limitless.

By contemplating, believing, and knowing who and what you really are, then your self-realization will draw you ever nearer to me. My grace is—as I explained earlier—abundant for you all. It is forever. When this is understood, both contentment and peace will reign inside and out of your heart. Remember to also let go of trepidation and fear. Each day, trusting you will receive exactly what you need at every moment. Have confidence in what you do, as this proves you also trust in yourself too.

I understand and realise that there are those days, weeks, months, and years where family, financial, work, and home commitments and responsibilities seem to demand most of your waking hours. However, try to find a few moments for both you and me.

Indeed, those fields of gold may often seem so far away, fading into the horizon, but the inner glow which will enable you to reap your own eternal harvest will never fade or die. So, remember we are always 'one', that you are already 'free', and that you have unimaginable power within you, too. Amen.

LESSON 31:
IMAGINE

In the words of the song (of the same title), can you imagine? Can you truly imagine a life without war, famine, and the world living as one, or are such times only in dreams, and for dreamers too? Well, please appreciate your thoughts (and your imagination), have a far greater importance than you may realise.

Understand they transcend both time and space in every dimension. They float upon the ether to drift high into the light, or they can swirl and sink into the murky recesses of the mind, which will reflect pain, anxiety, ego, and fear.

Similarly—as stated before—people will often believe 'you are what you eat'. But an even greater reality is through what you think and also say. The results of such can materialize moments, years, or even lifetimes away. Such things hang upon a knife edge. With so many choices and decisions, it is the intent and the intensity behind them which emits a positive or negative chain reaction, and therefore a resulting outcome.

Therefore, every being and species in their countless different forms are all affected by such an outcome. This brings victory or defeat, elation and joy, or even despair and desolation. Everything is so finely balanced, and without the foresight of truth and wisdom, those countless thoughts can appear almost identical.

Take an athlete, having trained for many years of their life with the desire to become an Olympic champion. Now try to imagine they have just made their dream come true. Their tears may instantaneously fall; a release of overwhelming joy in that realization … a culmination of perseverance, ambition, immense effort, and belief.

In contrast, someone finishing in second place may also cry, but with great sadness and sheer despondency. Perhaps, even stating that they have underachieved, let down those who had supported, encouraged, and helped to motivate them in their pursuit and goal. Maybe they would even say, "I didn't do my best."

It is difficult for many to comprehend those feelings of both the victory and so-called 'defeat'. However, as I am with and within you all, for whom are these emotional waters actually shed? Well, in every experience there are lessons to be learnt, and with those imaginary athletes, it is not only for themselves, but for those who have viewed such scenarios too. They can not only inspire a younger generation, but they can also motivate, lead, and provide others with a greater determination to succeed in many areas of both sport and life.

Remember, those receiving gold, silver, or bronze medals are not the only winners. All other participants are not just also-rans or losers. One must understand, just as I do not judge any such sporting event and/or any result as being more valuable than another, it should become easier to comprehend that you are all racing along in life … upon whatever course, profession, work, or role you have been granted or have chosen.

So, upon every pathway, what really matters is not just about a podium finish. The real victory lies in the effort which has been given freely, wantonly, and willingly in all shapes and forms. Then, if one should be fortunate to receive accolades, it is vital that ego does not come to the fore, raising its ugly head. Likewise, by being gracious—no matter where one is placed—dignity is maintained, and balance gained.

It is important, though, to remember some pitfalls of such successes. What do I mean? Well, for those with gold medals placed around their necks, what can—or do—they do next? After a performance which has highlighted their strengths and talents, will there be an after effect? In time, without continued adulation or having a new goal and purpose, one could become withdrawn or anxious. Depression can sometimes try to drag their love and light, hope and determination into the gutter.

Know that you cannot compare this to your own self- realization. This is the understanding of who and what you really are, and how you are all important members of society and humanity. So, in striving to achieve this greater goal, you only need to imagine yourself as being fearless. Trust in me to guide, teach, support, nurture, lead, and protect, leaving you just to believe in 'you'.

If you were a leaf upon a breeze, you would freely float and land where you will. Likewise, because you are a spark of divinity—which ignites and shines—you can bring light to all those in need, purposefully and righteously. All the while, you will remember you are not on your own, and never can be. Therefore, it does not matter where your physical body resides, or indeed where your soul and consciousness travels upon the layers of vibration and energy, either within or around you.

So then, in all your endeavours, please shy away from self-criticism. It is more often the case that no one else is judging you other than yourself. "He (or she) is faster, fitter, slimmer, better looking, has fewer problems, and is luckier than I am". Are you really so sure about these things?

Although it is sometimes difficult to count your blessings in the world and society in which you live today, it is very important you try to do so. If one is content (as I have stated many times before), then you are not sacrificing your time to just work for 'money'. You can use it to better oneself, your character and personality. You can show the reality of who you are ... not only as a person and a human being, but as a soul.

Appreciate this is not just about what one may give materially. It is the essence of your love 'within' ... which transcends through your smile, actions, thoughts, and words. These have a greater influence upon those whom you meet, and those who also seem a great distance from your physical presence.

Perhaps it is now a good time to take stock of your life. Think of where you are heading. What areas can you improve in your life? Perhaps it's personal, or with work, business, home and family. How about your relationship with yourself and also me (I am I)?

It is you and your heart which must prevail by your own virtues, to make the glory of love and truth reign as the true victor—for this is the main race and event which supersedes all others. At the end of your days (whenever this may come), you will each stand forever as your own champion, adorned by my eternal grace as an everlasting witness to the light. Is that so truly hard to imagine? Amen.

.

LESSON 32:
HURTING

Welcome once more. So, as the title implies, you may instinctively think of this in terms of the body. Or perhaps, even emotionally and mentally, but seldom one considers this subject spiritually.

Indeed, just like your physical form, which bleeds from an open wound, love too can drain from the heart. This may occur through spoken—or unspoken—words, having selfish thoughts, and via hateful, angry actions. Your soul will ache from indecision, and through the lack of contentment and control of the senses ... which ignites the fires of desire in so many more ways than one.

Therefore, the effect will always follow the cause. Once started, all one can hope to achieve is damage control in its various degrees. For instance, consider relationships or, more precisely, a marriage ... knowing that first and foremost, every element of life deserves to be happy, and any union is only as strong as its weakest link. Is that pressure? Does that create a greater responsibility for one over another?

These are human traits. When one realises true happiness stems only from within, then all will understand that any dissatisfaction comes not from another, but only from 'self'. You are all perfect, sparks of divinity, remember?

So then, visualize—if you can—betrayal or unfaithfulness, leading to a loss of trust, be it from a husband, wife, or partner. Would you blame, shout, or scream, or could one tear drop mean more than any words can say? (Remember, I am not your judge and jury, as I have always reiterated within these books.)

Simplicity is the key. This also provides the answers. One only has to consider if the action, thought, or word is from, through, and to love, being selfless in its manifestation, or whether it leads to indescribable pain.

Please do not bring self-worth into the equation. You derive no benefit from enquiring with the mind over whether one's own behaviour could have prevented such things. Blindness is not conducive to the eyes alone. In any case, some people will try to deceive anyone and anything, but all need to comprehend no one and no 'thing' can ever erase or hide the truth from me. So-called good, bad, or indifferent gestures, acts, thoughts, and words all leave a trace - no matter when, where, or how!

However, why should I mention all this? And for what purpose and outcome are these points raised? Well, first and foremost, one must question no other but themselves. It may seem instinctive to most … to want to condemn, chastise, and lash out against someone or something which has caused pain, anguish, fear, and trepidation. If you are ever in a situation which seems to impart these feelings upon you, step back in body, soul, and mind, even for just one moment. Try to view the scenario differently, as sometimes all is not what it appears or seems.

Such challenges in one's life may seem overwhelming. They can all provide a silver lining; it's only that you cannot see these straight away, or you take such experiences too literally and at face value. Try to believe then, every day can reveal golden nuggets of enlightenment, wisdom, and education for daily living, and for one's heart and soul's eternal glory.

I also understand why so many of you ask—and wish—me to provide or just meet every demand and prayer they make. I could, but how would you all grow? Please appreciate discussing the example of a strained or broken relationship is not a trivial one, as it is more like opening a whole can of worms. "Whose fault—your fault—my fault?"

Know I observe and have heard it all, in every dialect and upon every tongue. Jealousy, intimidation, dissatisfaction, and frustration with (or from) one another are just some traits to mention. "Your right—I'm wrong." "It is you—not me." "I've changed—you've changed." The list is endless.

But by holding truth in your heart and then displaying such through one's character and personality … in all resulting consequences, I will bear as the true witness to such. So, you just need to trust in yourself and in me.

Forgiveness, too, has its place. It can eliminate stress, angst, fear, and disease in an instant. It cannot be undertaken lightly or half-heartedly though. Even a still ocean has strong undercurrents which can swirl, disorientate, confuse, and carry one to disturbing areas of emotion and life.

No … one needs to be honest and true. This will keep you afloat by staying calm, no matter what the hurt may be. Understand then, love is both the door to eternal peace and a content life while in one's physical embodiment. And so, by deciding from, through, and to the heart—and not by the 'sense' induced mind—things which at first appear to overwhelm and appear of mountainous proportions will shrink. They'll reduce to manageable speed bumps as you progress upon your life's journey.

You are already free. So do not believe fate has ever trapped you, or that any place, or by the timing of your physical 'sojourn' upon the 'earth-plane' either. Only your own limitations can ever shackle your will, and power, and creative essence of your divinity.

Therefore, the world over, you can see those who are hurting physically, mentally, emotionally, and spiritually, but who then overcome and achieve both wonderful and everlasting moments of beauty and glory. They take life with encouragement, perseverance, fortitude, and determination, which transcend body and mind. These are lasting legacies, captured by memories of the heart and by love into eternity.

'There is no gain without pain' some say, and undoubtedly, the pain can actually show you are truly alive. No matter what type of shadow looms and attempts to hide your true light, know you can forever shine and illuminate your true reality. Know this can never be cajoled, abused, burnt, broken, or destroyed ... because you are from my heart, and will always be! Amen.

LESSON 33:
SOMETIMES

When all around you seems to pass you by—at what feels like a million miles an hour—sometimes you just need to 'be'. I bear witness to each day rolling into the next, with one's 'chores', duties, and those responsibilities of work, family, friends (as well as the home) which insist your attention. Life can be a constant rush or blur, with the mind engaged and ceaselessly thinking of the next minute, hour, day, week, month, and year ahead.

So, just for a while, can you place the exterior on hold, pressing an imaginary pause button upon the day's tasks, in order for some 'time-out'? I do not—and will not—encourage the waste of any second or minute, but explain that within the stillness of your heart, one can re-learn and experience each new day. One can chose to feel more alive, and in doing so grow to know thyself (and I) in greater and more meaningful ways.

Do not be dismayed (or disturbed) by lists of things to accomplish or problems to solve, people to meet, places to go, or by the inconvenient sounds made by 'man', or man-made impermanent things. Try to de-clutter the mental horizon.

Focus instead upon nature, and those natural sounds around you … like birdsong, insects buzzing, and the rustling of leaves. Or, if you should open your eyes, try gazing out towards passing clouds and those birds in flight, and the butterflies and bees resting on nearby flowers. You could even go outside … to feel the sunshine on your face. It will surely lift your spirit and cast off many burdens from your shoulders.

Please also understand, true peace reigns not in the time between wars, but in the letting go of everything you think or feel you were, are, or can ever become. So too, just as I have stated before, if you wish to 'enjoy', then simply end your search for 'joy'.

Realise and appreciate most people who strive to feel happy require the next thrill or so-called 'high' from sensory pleasures, but these are only fleeting. One then has to deal with the periods of time between them. However, by treating pleasure and pain with the same indifference, no angst or depression can set in. The after effect of excitement will simply drain away and disperse, like water through a sieve.

In contrast, within moments of contemplation—along with periods of togetherness and harmony between family and friends—peace stays constant. It remains captured like a photograph, becoming etched into your heart and soul forever. These are the special times, and the energy and vibration of their essence, one can remember and cherish more easily.

Appreciate your love and my love is one which permeates all things. It is everlasting. So, how do you come to know and live this? Well, first, you need to recognize it. For example, imagine the fragrance of a flower, and by doing so, you'll understand you do not need to see or touch the flower itself to experience this. Simplicity is the key, and it must always remain this way, remember.

You understand the difference between night and day; dark and light, wrong or right (unless the mind is impaired through or by the body) don't you? As a result, all life knows the source of love deep within, and hence, love knows all.

Love is the only permanent thing in all creation. So, why must you worry almost every day? The world keeps spinning, the sun will continue to shine, and the rain will fall, and where life is born, it inevitably dies. Indeed, the period within physical embodiment is brief. Only your love, character, and personality will leave traces across the sands of time. These cannot fade, unlike the memories of those who are still earthbound, as they remain a part of you, your soul, and very being.

Understand and believe too, we are all connected. We cannot be separated by the exterior illusion and confusion which surrounds—and wishes—to invade what you think is your personal 'space'. It is only by making a conscious effort to grasp who and what you are—and can yet become through self-realization—that enables you to experience true stillness and inner growth in silence.

How many times have you ever said aloud, "I can't hear myself think in here", citing noise, loud talking, or music? It is the same with listening and conversing with each other. Can you really hear me when your body or mind is forever engaged in work or play?

Therefore, when you're inside the stillness, you will feel, sense, and also know the answers you seek. This will become more clearly defined than ever before. Believe then that I am waiting for you. I am ready at all times, for I am within, without, beside, above, below, and am everywhere and in everything. Hence, you become able to trust me to always provide you with whatever you need (but not necessarily with what you think you want ... or when).

Please, do not wait for 'life' to become just a little too much to bear before you seek me—as so often is the case through fear, pain or loss—because you can call to me when you feel happy, relieved, and are glad, too!

Life always continues. Therefore, acknowledge and look forward to those times when everything around you needs to carry on, but you (as if disappearing from everyone else's view) must sometimes just simply 'be'. Amen.

LESSON 34:
LONGING

I long for you, though I am not weak, and I yearn for those moments when you are aware of our connection in mind, body, and soul. So, please do not fear any false separation or division. Know that you will remember all hearts are 'one'—always and in all ways—if you would but only recognize me, and more importantly, recognize your true 'self'.

Therefore, within peacefulness, a wavering soul will find the truth. Like an irregular heartbeat, it will then steady itself in the knowingness of who, what, and why it exists. Likewise—and in a constant rhythm—the energy and vibration of you all is eternal. Therefore, it becomes easier to comprehend all life merges throughout and, on the ether, beyond time and space, and every dimension.

However, within your soul's journey, there will be occasions where one seems to drift along through days and nights, wondering about your purpose and the design of all things which you think you know and love. One may long for information and need guidance. Or, even question how and why you often feel the way you do.

So then, try to imagine a husband and wife, or two lovers kept seemingly apart by circumstance, or perhaps by so-called fate or divine intervention. They may even wait for a letter or phone call, perhaps one that provides a message of hope for the other. Indeed, they miss each other's company. In this absence, they long to hear loving words, feel a gentle touch or tender kisses. Hearts may ache, hunger wanes, desire multiplies, and longing intensifies.

Upon every level—emotionally, mentally, physically, and spiritually—such things touch you and can transform one's well-being instantaneously. So, it is vital to maintain balance in all that's said and done. One may think of 'attachments', but as we have discussed this before, we will not dwell upon it here. Appreciate your true attachment goes way beyond any physical desire and for (or because of) any impermanent 'thing'.

Remember, it is love which transcends all such instances. Any real or imaginary walls or barriers cannot contain it. Therefore, in longing to connect, whether to any other soul (or even to me), appreciate true love flies upon hopes, dreams, and wishes, and those thoughts of such. They stand out like beacons burning brightly in a night sky, like brilliant suns amongst the stars, or vibrant rainbows across the horizon, and even those tears which roll down a face. All leave their traces and tracks of sincerity ... because they shine purposefully, being selfless in design.

In contrast, ill thoughts for another or those which long for self-gratification and a false desire (being of a selfish intent), stand out in other ways. They resemble a bruise upon the skin, or longer lasting upon the ego, causing greater pain, and suffering. More serious are those like tattoos or deep scars, which leave a more permanent marker, etched not on the body but within. Only by balancing and erasing karma, with—and through—love and truth, can these fade ... which then allows the soul to bloom with the fragrance of purity and an essence of divinity.

So, ask yourself, what do you long for right now? Is it material in its construction, perhaps for a car, new home, or latest 'tech' or appliance? What about for a holiday, more money, or even what you think could make a more comfortable life?

Of course, there is absolutely nothing wrong with striving to achieve your goals. But it is far better to gain greater knowledge, experience, and even more responsibility, whether that is in (or at) one's work, rest, or play. All these can provide the drive and determination to achieve what you need ... or sometimes what you think you want.

Now, moving on from this, consider those who long for simpler things. Finding a job and being able to provide for their family ... or, perhaps for a roof over their head, for food and water, and to just having a good friend. When you think about these, can you still feel that there is something missing in your relationships, your work, home, or general existence? If so, please stop this right now. Understand negativity attempts to infiltrate your mind, creeping up upon you like a thief in the night.

Realise—by believing in me—that I am I ... that 'God' exists, and we are all 'one'. ... It will be much easier to comprehend and live knowing you are already free, and that you have the power to mould the way you think, and live and feel every single day. You can bend, shape, and create—both inside and out—the life you need, because you are part of creation, not separate from it. Indeed, you co-create, not only through 'self' ... but with each other, and of course, through me. So, please trust me, and it will follow you'll then trust in yourself ... to reach your full potential, both as a human being and as a soul.

Okay then, even though I started this lesson by stating 'I long for you', do not be confused into thinking that what I have spoken about today actually contradicts this. Let me suggest something. Does a parent not long for their child or children to be strong, healthy, kind, generous, prosperous, faithful, trustworthy, friendly, and a credit to the family? Well, you are all my 'children'. You are part of me for all eternity. So, how can this 'relationship' be any different? (Only you can answer this.)

Know that there is so much each of you can achieve. You can lighten and enlighten the world, and far beyond it. You can make a difference, and only fear can deny or hold you back. Why? Because fear restricts and hinders ambitions. It places obstacles which seem like immovable mountains in your path, causing one's energy to dissipate and weaken, to the point of accepting defeat in pursuit of personal or global goals.

In contrast when you focus upon love, which glorifies the divinity inside you, problems become challenges. Anger and hatred turn to forgiveness. Your life will take on a whole new meaning and perspective. Hurting another will be far from your mind and helping others will become the greater focus of one's daily existence.

Through your own self-realization, the truth will bring contentment closer to your heart. Then, it will be much easier to find bliss and peace within and out. This will help to prevent such longing for all other things … all of which have less meaning and purpose upon your own road to victory and everlasting life over death. Amen.

LESSON 35:
SERVICE

Welcome to every heart, all of which (I hope) are now opened to see, hear, or feel these words today. May they all float through the ether and fall—like leaves upon a breeze—onto the land. They will arrive exactly and precisely where I meant them to, both for the individual, and for all those who gather in the name of love, light, and truth.

So, though I have spoken many times before regarding 'service', and why each one of you should love and serve all, I must ask you directly, how do you actually feel about serving another? Is it gratefully, willingly, and wantonly? Or are you somehow reluctant and find it regrettable to do so? Indeed, one may even feel they have become a servant in their daily, weekly, and monthly tasks, but can you say that this is a negative or a positive scenario?

Although many societies have changed over recent generations, there are those who still work as 'servants' today. Perhaps this is for heads of state or even royalty, though these are few compared to the overall population of the world. To get a true picture, one must look at these scenarios, not just from the outside looking in, but from the viewpoint of both the so-called 'master and servant' themselves.

For some, it may all seem demeaning. The mind will insist that the role of a servant leads to anger, jealousy, and frustration. These thoughts only bring separation to human beings. It implies there are those who have … and then there's the have 'not's' … people of a supposed higher class, who are deemed above those who are not fit for any other purpose.

That said, many others did—or still do—see a servant's role as an opportunity to experience a new environment. In fact, by witnessing places or people they normally wouldn't see, they realise it is a way and means to improve oneself. Perhaps, by creating a better standard of living, not only for themselves, but for their families, too.

Like most areas of people's lives, it is the ego which dictates one's thoughts and actions. So, the role you play within the theatre of life upon the Earth actually bears no relation or consequence. When you are all born equal (please dismiss money, physicality, and gender) and have the same divine essence within you, then no one should be seen as being—or working—

above or below one's 'station'. Do you (or have you) ever felt this way?

You will always feel happy if you enjoy what you do, and not take the role that you play as being just a means to an end. I know this, as sometimes family responsibilities, work, or a lack of money forces a person to take on new, unfamiliar work … or have life-changing circumstances thrust upon them. But please understand, such times as these give rise to new opportunities. They are not always doom and gloom. Remember, you are never alone. So, once again, I state you do not need to fear, for I know exactly what you need, and when.

One should not worry about the whys, what's and wherefores. Simply do the best you can. After all, those in the so-called menial job still get served too, be it in the shop, store, or a restaurant, for example. Therefore, who is serving who the most? You all serve each other without even thinking or believing it. So, it is natural to assist and help each other, even if one doesn't realise it! Therefore, you are still serving 'God', as everyone is a spark of divinity and me.

Any fruits of your labour should become secondary. Please do not constantly worry about this respect. Of course, it becomes harder to do if you are below or on the 'breadline'. Try you must, for anxiety and angst display a lack of trust in yourself and also in me. Such negativity attempts to block the ways ahead in which I am to lead and guide you forward.

By supporting yourself and each other, no human being should struggle to survive. Nor should they have too little (or nothing) to eat or drink. By sharing and serving all life, then all of life can serve you, too. For example, Mother Earth freely gives all her resources to humanity. Likewise, the light of the sun. Both are constant and unwavering whilst they support, serve, and help humanity to survive, grow, and experience. Do they 'speak', requesting anything in return? No. Do they stop shinning or provide the sustenance you require with any condition attached? No.

Only through your love can you realise and appreciate the joy of warmth, the air that you breathe, the water you drink and cleanse your body with, the clothes you make—or buy—to wear, the fuel you get for your home, the beautiful sunsets and sunrises, and the mountains, lakes, seas, fire and ice. All these things in creation are for you. Know that I serve you gladly … and eternally.

So, may you understand, 'service' goes way beyond each day in which you rise from your bed … to who you work for, and the reasons behind all your tasks. Everything is linked—inevitably, uniquely, and specifically—for the benefit of every being and soul. Therefore, every relationship in work, rest, and play provides a benefit and lesson. No matter how small or large and whatever form this takes, it might not be apparent at the time, or even until years later.

You may all question the purpose, but not the experience or outcome. You will always grow in knowledge through it, which therefore leads you to gain wisdom. Be certain that it can carry you forward upon the path you—your soul—had chosen ... way before one's physical embodiment upon the 'earth-plane.'

Understand and appreciate then, whether you are knee deep in rubbish, living life in the gutter, or if your body lies upon silk sheets and your head appears to live amongst the stars ... know it is all temporary, fleeting, and impermanent.

Only your heart and soul contain the humility to overcome the smugness of false power and ego. Or those unwanted depths and lows of what seems an unworthiness of self, carried towards your fellow 'man'. True service must, therefore, start with love. Not for self-gain or in pity either, but because it will enable you to elevate the oneness of you all, now and forever. Amen.

LESSON 36:
FOG

Welcome to one and all. May you truly sense and know your own truth inside your heart. This will enable you to strive forward, becoming enriched with fortitude, courage, and conviction. And help to achieve one's goal of self-realization into bliss and eternal peace.

However, at this precise moment in time, many nations, hearts, and souls have become blinded. This resembles their earthly vision being impeded by low-lying fog. It has been slowing down, encapsulating, and praying upon imaginary fears and dread. Therefore, one could easily become suppressed by becoming overly cautious, lest a trip or fall render you lost and lonely. Or worse still, allow the mind to believe such illusion and confusion can deny me and the truth of whom and what you actually are.

That said, I do not intend to give a lecture or lesson to those in the world regarding how fog is formed and created. It is only the symptoms that mirror the same human traits ... which lead to either weakness or strength, and victory or defeat.

So, please understand you can train yourself to overcome negativity. The love which flows through you can distinguish between what is real and what is false. With love, one may observe the deceit and lies of human nature. Like an overcast shadow which attempts to obscure your view, it also reveals those selfless actions that provide hope and goodwill toward many aspects of life all around you.

Comprehend too, in challenging times, dense fog may descend upon your clear thinking. This can frustrate, hinder, and make you believe you are stuck, rooted to the spot, unable to see your hand in front of your face. The easiest decision would be to wait, keep still, and draw upon your divine essence within you. Comprehend that inside what you call the body is 'I', the eternal witness and spark of light more powerful than your mind could ever imagine.

As I often state, when you see with—and through—the mind, heart, and soul as one, then all barriers, either real or unreal, crumble before you. This, of course, is easier when you have faith. Though you may immediately think of this as being one of the many religions to help guide you towards the truth. I do not mean this. It is in having a very real belief and trust in yourself. When you have instilled this within your heart, you'll have faith in me, an automatic consequence of acknowledging the love and light inside your heart and soul.

In an instance, all darkness—and any fog or shadow having crept upon you—can be dispelled. Just like a curtain or veil drawn open to reveal a new and brilliant sunrise and dawn, light will permeate and dissolve trepidation, crush fear ... and banish hate and anger from lips and hearts.

If you can believe this to be true, then your life's irritations will be fleeting. Problems will become merely challenges that are overcome more quickly, for I can work through you with greater ease. With internal and external barriers laid down through your thoughts, words, and deeds, then your road opens up before you with new clarity and purpose. You can move forward with meaning, integrity, and honesty, in the knowing you do not need to worry if something is wrong, for it will always feel 'right'.

In fact, I see so many people start their day wondering whether their decisions they have made—and their actions taken—could or should have been different. But when you act with truth from the heart, then whatever is said or done is always correct. Consequences and results may give cause for concern, but I promise you they are not your burden. One's own karmic imbalance cannot be added to this way.

On the other side of the coin, if one plots to hurt and maim, attempting to leave hearts, bodies, and minds broken ... who do you think has to compensate or pay for it? People, upon hearing an old joke, will often state, "The old ones are the best". Well, so too are those with a serious note ... 'So shall you sow, and so shall you reap', though this should not place any fear into those with hearts of truth.

So where do you feel you're at right now? Over the last few days, weeks, months, or years, can you see more clearly in the direction you are headed? Do you have the awareness to stride towards a new horizon? If so, are you becoming more comfortable with the steps you're taking, the people you meet, and life's tasks that come your way? Alternatively, are your hands outstretched in front of you, waving them side to side, trying to grasp and hold on to something familiar, whilst looking for a chink of light?

Please appreciate, too, that each of you has your own life to lead and karma to erase or balance, even though we are all part of each other. Therefore, even though your own decisions (be it in work, rest, or play) can influence a single person—or even the many—one still cannot eradicate or increase another's karma, either willingly or mistakenly.

People will often feel that chaos reigns everywhere. But what I state actually reveals it is only love which brings 'order'. It unites—and never divides—humanity ... and all beings across every dimension, throughout space and all time.

Understand too, I realise that some days your life may seem so very tough. It is even more so for those who are hungry, thirsty, or without a home. So then, know this fog may often appear to linger physically over you, emotionally within you, and spiritually inside and out of you, but it is precisely these times that through your endurance, you will strengthen your character. Then, you will gain hope to achieve all you need and so very much more.

Keep believing, keep trying, and keep forgiving. The light will radiate, shine, and guide you through every barrier, real or unreal and seen or unseen. Remember, I am with you; I am you - and we are one for all eternity. Amen.

LESSON 37:
BURN

The phoenix will rise from the ashes, make no mistake of that. Humanity will then realise the truth, the oneness of all things. When it does, hatred, pain, anguish, and fear will burn like fierce flames upon a funeral pyre.

I mention these things to make the reader, listener, and the writer of these words take head. And, to notice that change is coming more quickly than anyone of you can comprehend. As such, when all have gained bliss and peace through their own self-realization, each individual (like sparks rising from the embers of a log fire) will fly into eternity with, from, and through my loving heart.

Please know then that I cradle every one of you. Each soul is deep inside of me; you are that precious, just like a teardrop, to become the jewels in my crown of Universal truth.

Understand those tarnished by darkness and shadow—of one's own making during many incarnations of flesh and bone—will have more than just begun their new journey. In the years to come, the world's population will change their opinions of each other, with family, friends, and neighbours no longer becoming motivated by ego, or having individual quests for any material gain.

Thus, an inner desire to care, protect, and nurture life will fill every heart, lifting the energy of the planet to greater heights. Mother Earth will blossom and bloom like no one has ever seen before, because harmony between humanity will shine and radiate far and wide.

For some, this will seem so farfetched. Even a quantum leap of faith cannot imagine it. For others, these are the words they have been waiting for all of their lives. They were hoping and wishing that somehow and sometime, everything could change. Tears of sadness, not just for loved ones, but for the animals, insects, and flora which are all as important within my kingdom, will turn to ecstasy … with such joy, tears of laughter and being pain free. I will encompass and sustain all.

You just need to keep on believing in the good that you do, and in those who do 'good' for you. Somehow, someday, it will all be over—this so-called waiting for 'me'. Know that however close to the edge of doubt you seem to think you are (or can ever become), I am with you, beside you, inside of you, out of you, and am you. So please, please, please do not ask or say, "I want to know what love is". You are in love. I am love. We are both one and the same.

This being the case, no matter what you face, whatever pain or heartache you seem to go through, all is fleeting compared to our eternal connection. Yes, I do witness all hurtful times. So many of your hearts become emotionally drained by rejection, or from the apparent loss of a loved one, too. 'Bodies' appear to be broken through fear, anger, crime, and war; minds snapped from a lack of support or forgiveness; and the soul's light of a thousand suns is covered and cast under a shadow of past deeds, regrets, and failed dreams.

Know it is then that I hold your hand. I whisper in your ear. I am the seeds of positive thought you can feel and hear when you pass and wade through the clutter of this impermanent world ... in which your physical sojourn now resides.

So, I ask you not to fade, not when you are so close to living the dream, the truth of all things. Please push forward. Keep moving. Do not rest upon your laurels but keep reaching out ... and let your love 'light' the way ahead for you and for the many. Indeed, all those who walk the pathway of illumination leave a trail, like stardust cast from my hand in the beginning of creation ... with each soul a tiny speck, yet still sparkling in the ether, against a backdrop of doubt and despair.

Other souls will follow. They will learn and grow from new knowledge and experience, gaining wisdom to the truth within them. I will attract each one of you to me, just as a magnet draws iron fillings across a page. Not because I force you, but because you want to. Love knows no bound. So, even in the darkest of days, and no matter how far you believe you have drifted from me, I am still here and there and everywhere.

I may seem to be the tiniest, faintest chink of light at the end of the tunnel, but I am I ... always, and for all times. Therefore, you are not lost. The darkness has not, and never will, 'win' ... because it is only a reflection of the same light within and without all things that exist, including you and me.

Let no one tell you any differently, so believe in what your heart tells you. It will never let you down. Then, if or when you feel confused, or ever despair, I will be the voice of your conscience to guide you through barricades which others (or even yourself) erect to keep me from you ... and from you knowing me and the truth 'inside'.

Our love will burn away every false desire. It will also keep you warm on those days when you feel frozen by indecision and uncertainty. It is the one fuel which cannot erode or ever dissolve ... unlike the natural resources deep within the Earth being consumed by humanity, and which will eventually dissipate and be no more.

Indeed, it is the most powerful, sustainable energy, for it cannot be bought, bargained for, manipulated, bent, or broken against its will. Any other force cannot contain love and hence it is permanent, going beyond the veil of so-called death. It is the greatest gift I give to you in order that you will grow and learn, and then realise you have only come full circle … back unto yourself. Amen.

LESSON 38:

SHIPS

You are a 'vessel', floating upon the ocean of my love. However, do not compare yourself with a ship that moves under, over, or through the world's seas. Those ships need man-made power to propel them forward, or they are fortunate to benefit from the wind—an asset of nature—to help guide them where they wish to go.

No, you are different; unique because your true light is the buoyancy, which helps steer you through testing times and journeys, and it enables you to bear witness to the truth. So, try to imagine and compare the seas upon the earth with the real sea of tranquillity, bliss, and peace. In doing so, you will recognize one's own freedom, for you would then understand that even driftwood does not travel aimlessly.

Indeed, you are not like Christopher Columbus, having a belief that one day you might sight land, ready for hope and glory. No, for in spiritual terms, the discovery is not of—or even for—a place, which appears to rise above the horizon, but it is instead of, and for, your true selves. Therefore, just like circumnavigating around the globe, one will always come full circle, but it is through the sojourns of life and experience that you'll finally realise you have simply returned to self.

Know then, experiencing challenges is no more than the under-currents of your existing journey, which attempt to lure you away from your present course. That said, some will only nudge you gently from side to side. Others, fanned by an inflamed mind—being manipulated by the senses or via one's ego—will attempt to rock and capsize you (stifling true growth, whilst inflicting pain on yourself and others), or even worse still, drag you under, submerging you with deep regrets.

So, I ask you, when you read or see so-called 'bad' news across the planet, and feel perplexed, dismayed, angry, or confused, are you able to sympathize and empathize and yet still (somehow) distinguish between fact and fiction, and the true reality of living within (or without) love? What I state may give cause for serious consideration, and rightly so, but how many people see their life differently to this, as if leisurely sailing across a boating lake?

On the surface, this seems fine. But when viewed with and through the lens of truth, not only does it restrict and inhibit one's experiences, it also has a knock on effect to those who know and live with them ... though how can this be so?

To comprehend this, start by picturing a boating lake 'scene' within your mind. It has very few vessels upon it. The water is almost always calm, being sheltered by the land which surrounds it. Hence, the experience will usually be a familiar one. You encounter the same scenes and move across the same emotional water time after time. Would you not agree that it may well appear to be the easier, safer option ... but it offers little, with no 'new' knowledge? This leads to stifled experiences and also generates a lack of wisdom.

Therefore, one should dispense with the idea of trying to get through one's life devoid of challenges. Confidence grows when you embark upon the richness of change. After all—as for all souls born onto the 'earth-plane', this is not your maiden voyage, where you could easily feel trepidation or have grave concerns about reaching a destination.

However, there are still so many people who often think that they are born, they live and then they die. Yet this would be like a bon voyage, only wishing to have a good time ... then strangely jumping ship before it's ready to dock. What would be the point of it?

If there wasn't one, then most people would just steal, have no conscience, and be unethical; a racist, as well as becoming unkind, lying, cheating, hating, and believe me, this type of list is endless. Fortunately, the majority do not do (and are not) these things. Because love, in whatever shape or form you imagine it to be, is prevalent in all life. It can be seen, felt, heard, and known 'within', unless the mind has been impaired through illness, or has deteriorated with (or from) abuse of the physical.

So then, what about your future conduct, not just towards others, but towards yourself and even me? As you make your way (and from this day forward), will you try to avoid feeling—or facing—the truth? Are we to be like ships, which pass each other by in the night?

The answer, of course, is no. So please understand what I say, no matter how difficult life gets. By turning within your heart, you will always cruise into safer, calmer waters. My loving arms, like a harbour (which span across every dimension throughout the ether, space, and all time), remain open to you, welcoming you to draw breath and rest if you need to.

If you let me, I will always steer you in the right direction. If you trust me, I will help you navigate through those waves of pressure which repeatedly crash against your body, mind and soul. These only serve as reminders, though ... to help you chose and make the right decisions.

Indeed, you will learn from past mistakes. You can embrace the future, not with uncertainty, but with continued enthusiasm and determination, sharing the true you. Others will then see the same happiness and spark of light inside themselves.

Keep in mind; you can recognize me as the wind within your sail, and as the power inside you. I am the engine of motivation. Appreciate I will always be within, without, above, below, and beside you upon your journey. Hence, the vessel, no matter what your shape, colour, and size, is perfect, having every ingredient to succeed in its current experience. Therefore, always be yourself. By being true to self, others will see the same truth, which is in you, is inside of themselves too.

Like a flotilla of ships, each of you may appear different in looks and appearance, but you can all undertake the journey of self-realization with no fear or prejudice. Indeed, all these vessels (bodies) may carry flags, displaying different nationalities. Or perhaps show it affiliated them to various religions or faiths. Some may even carry the skull and crossbones to induce fear or death. Realise some can even temporarily travel away from the light, but as I see all things, there is no darkness or any depths which can disguise—or hide—every soul from me.

One day, every vessel will comprehend their true direction and purpose. It is only a matter of 'time'. After all, every ship has their anchor eternally attached to my heart. This is why you can never be lost or cast adrift … but will forever sail with me upon the ocean of my love. Amen.

LESSON 39:
HOLDING ON

If you can look with (and through) the lens of your heart, you will see me both 'within' and 'out' of you. Then, you would surely feel me as the gentle nudge of your conscience, be it with a thought or a whisper, yet shouting you to remember 'us' as 'one' together. As such, through the depths of confusion and illusion, you'll sense a hand reaching for you ... for it is I who urges you forward, towards the light.

So right now, imagine your outstretched palm grasping mine. Like a child holding its parent's hands, you will feel safe, cared for, and once more you will trust in the grip of protection and guidance from love up above. Trust and believe that I won't let go. I will not let you drift away into the darkness ever again, for those days have gone.

As I lift you up into my loving arms, I cradle you and bathe you with my grace, which will forever cleanse your soul. Then, as I lift you even higher, you're able to survey far beyond the horizon of the mortal coil into which you were reborn ... to bear witness to all of creation.

In your mind, you think you are infinitesimal, but in your heart, you'll realise you are everything and everything is you. With this belief comes balance. Then, through wisdom, comes the understanding that every soul is like a brilliant star, which can become even more beautiful by being cleansed from its journey through time. All will then value 'time', as it helps to remove the dust and debris of past thoughts and deeds. These have prevented one's own illumination from being discovered through your many previous bodily incarnations and life experiences.

I continue to watch you, as you survey the amazing vista of the Universe ... and so much more. So, do not feel sad or downhearted, thinking you are unimportant or even inconsequential, because as I have stated before, in the grand scheme of things, even a single grain of sand (upon a beach or desert) is vital, for it makes one whole.

So, what you now feel, see, and sense is nothing more than what I made you of. We can make no separation between the physical, spiritual, mental, and ethereal 'bodies', because you are totality, and can be nothing more and nothing less.

Your mind, though, may often try to disguise this truth from you ... in an attempt to show you are on your own, divided from me. But you are never alone and cannot be. Unlike a lost memory, of a forgotten name or face, you'll want to remember who and what you truly are. In searching for your answers, it will lead you towards self-realization. Then, inside your heart, you will sense something so much more than a simple daily 'existence'; so much so that the eureka moment will not be too long or far away.

Understand those previous months and years which have passed have not been wasted. They have enabled you to be where you are now. Therefore, with reading—or by hearing—these words, know they have not reached you upon a wish or a prayer; or by any 'chance' … for everything has its purpose and reason for being. Every moment can also be a 'lesson' in which to grow, become fulfilled, and to share and shine the love from within. So, will you grasp it then, just like you did my hand?

Comprehend this love I speak of is unconditional; it is selfless and also free from pain and disdain. Remember, it will rise like a phoenix from those ashes of deceit (which have tried to deceive you), enriching your life beyond any material or immaterial gain.

Know, too, that there are no precious metals or jewels upon the Earth—or indeed upon any other planet—which radiates like the core of your soul. Such words as it being majestic or brilliant could never do justice to this truth. Therefore, it is far better to spend your time contemplating how best to live, sharing the goodness of your heart upon your road to bliss.

Please, do not ask me how far you have travelled, or how much further you need to go, but continue to grow in confidence I am with you every step of the way. We breathe and live as one. Hence, I feel what you feel, see what you see, and ride the peaks and troughs of your so-called good and bad times, too.

Continue to trust in yourself and me, as your dream of eternal peace is but a heartbeat away. I am not a keeper of an imaginary doorway—which lies hidden—beyond your hopes and dreams. So, I'll remind you … you are the lock and the key, and one's heart is the true doorway into eternity.

Appreciate everything else fades or changes shape or form. This is because energy can be manipulated, bent, pushed, and pulled into (or because of) lower or higher vibrations or frequencies. In contrast, the love which you are is constant. It cannot be crushed, burnt, buried, or eroded, and that's why it is the very fabric of creation. True love remains throughout time, both within or 'out' of space and across every dimension. It is, of course, the very foundation of life and of you and me.

By holding on to this premise, you will also that it is the pillar stone of humanity, being the one and only 'religion' connecting all of humankind. That said, like the different colours, languages, shapes, and sizes of 'man', there are countless different faiths to help guide and educate the people of the world. So, all can grow as human beings and valued members of society, no matter where you each find yourselves.

However, we are still 'one. Yes, one God, one light, one love, and for any man or nation to attempt to divide us by negative thoughts, words, and deeds, they will surely fail. Such evil holds onto hate, anger, and fear, which also tries to disrupt and inflict doubt, anguish, and pain upon anyone or anything.

In contrast, my love is not discriminatory. It is there for every living thing. Some say it is often hidden, but clearly, this is not so. Love cascades like crystal waterfalls when a nation is grieving ... its people united, when loss or tragedy strikes or shakes it to its core. Such occasions show immense strength and bring forth depths of courage and character.

Indeed, landscapes across the globe are sometimes comprehensively altered. However, during every diversity and challenge you face, remember that I am holding on to you, and I will never, ever let you go. Amen.

LESSON 40:
RHYTHM

I hear your heartbeat. Like a drum, it beats to a regular rhythm, which echoes across time, space, and all dimensions. So, you may well ask, if I connect all hearts to mine, how could I possibly hear any one individual soul over the collective thoughts and feelings of billions, and all the elements of life?

Well, know that it is easy, for even though you are more intricate than any fragment of your DNA, you are all unique. Therefore, your soul's divine essence and light resonate to and from me with such simplicity that recognition is instantaneous. It is no more complex than knowing parts of my 'self', as I live within each one of you, remember? So, we are one (as I keep reiterating), and you are never alone no matter if you are held in a vice like grip by your greatest fear ... or are enjoying many of the pleasures of living.

As I feel and sense and hear those imaginary lows and highs, please try to treat both with equanimity. This will enable you to treat criticism and praise in the same vain. It will also bring balance through and from your being, which consequently reduces and then eradicates the ego ... which serves only hate, anger, and pain. It would be wise to dispel and remove this as soon as possible.

Indeed, it has no place in the rhythm of life, as will try to deny my working with—and through—you. Only egoism refuses to believe that the 'doer' of your actions can only be for, and from, your 'self'. In relation to this, one should consider your actions are only karmic, which manifests in every avenue ... all walks of life, and in all 'beings'. In fact, you could go as far to say karma is the creator of life, giving cause for many births to the 'earth-plane' throughout the history of one's soul.

Do not misunderstand what you read, hear, or comprehend about this. By now you have grown to realise that no matter what the reasons for one's rebirth to the physical and impermanent world may be, it is love and only love which ultimately sustains and transcends your energy to permanent peace. This is the truest desire, need, and goal of your soul.

So, do you feel you are repeatedly walking or travelling on the same old track, or have you recognized the junction ahead? Are you now ready—and prepared—to make the change(s) to feel fulfilled? And also share the beauty of life and love within you, to all whom you encounter on a new and different course?

Like a signal, I have always given you the green light to be whom you were born (and where you need) to be. Therefore, you need to recognize you have had these choices all along, but have previously denied who, what, and why you live and exist.

It is not to satisfy worldly desires, for they only bring further 'attachments'… shackling and restricting you from fulfilling your true self and being. Such things can spiral out of control, and only attempt to divert you away from the path of truth. When one becomes worried, it can lead to stress, disease, or depression if left unchecked.

Try to be content by living in the present, then the concerns of the past—and for the future—disappear. This is not a course or route where if one fails to plan, then you plan to fail … it is quite the opposite! When you regain control of your thoughts, words, and deeds, then the 'right' action prevails. It is only 'goodness', in terms of what is seen, felt, or heard, which ensues … not just for yourself, but for those around you, too.

Please understand, throughout one's journey, you can eradicate bad karma, just like a poison. Now compare this with the body. At least once in your life you would have been ill, becoming sick in the stomach. In such circumstances, these are the toxins which your body needs to remove, and which cause you to throw up.

In such an instance, you should not take medicine to stop you feeling nausea; it is only afterwards this should be taken. This is because when the negativity and imbalance have been removed, one may feel weak, but then healing can begin. Similarly, with the ego I mentioned earlier, it will cling like poisonous ivy, but in removing it will only strengthen you, and thus lead you onto greater things.

This does not differ from those trials and tribulations you face in various degrees. Many of you perhaps state I must say that you each deserve what you get (which may sound harsh), but it is down to you, the individual, to either accept or deny what you feel within your own heart. Remember, only you can question the validity and 'experience' of such.

It is the same with disagreements and arguments; anger is not transferred when one stays calm, and replies are given in whispers. You cannot work the flame of ego into a frenzy. This gives the one who remains within equanimity the true power, and also peace; indeed, it is a heavenly peace. The contaminants of hate, frustration, and fear are not digested within the mind. Therefore, further imbalance is not taken on board. If one remains doubtful of such, then simply try this when a disagreement (in its various layers and forms) lands upon your door. This is not a game but living within the true rhythmic state and energy of love.

Which brings me back full circle, and once more to our eternal connection. So, throughout the Universe you can hear me, and the frequencies of light and sound which scientists track with radio waves are no more than all of what we are: creation.

Indeed, people continually state there must be life 'out there', or totally assume otherwise; by thinking they can only find intelligent life upon the Earth. However, there are countless planets and beings, more than the stars you bear witness to in the night sky. Currently, humankind cannot 'see' the whole truth, or beyond the dimension of time and space in which you all live. So, to fully appreciate and understand the marvel of it all, then one must first turn within. It is the only way.

Therefore, when you connect with me in your heart, the truth becomes known. In seeing and believing you are a spark of divinity; it is easier to comprehend that a soul is the real 'star'. As such, the answers are all inside every one of you. Amen.

LESSON 41:
SUSTENANCE

Sustenance of what, you might well ask! Well, this lesson will hopefully explain and guide you, telling you what can help you physically, mentally, and spiritually. Therefore, strength and conviction are maintained, which enables the achievement of one's goals … and fulfils the purpose of your being.

Know too, the body, mind, and soul (of you all) are very complex in their structure and makeup. And yet are also simplistic in nature, for they all need to grow and learn … having an inbuilt desire not only to survive, but to truly 'live'. You will also see how they are all interconnected and affect each other greatly.

First, please understand the greatest gift the body can receive is sleep. Think of how nice it would feel to lay your head upon a soft pillow, stretching out in a bed of fresh cotton or silk sheets, whilst being wrapped up in blankets made of wool … or perhaps feather duvets. Then, consider how such rest can help provide you with the energy for your daily tasks. In stark contrast, without sleep, the body degenerates, weakening at a rapid rate. Not only this, but it will also have an adverse effect upon the mind.

People often state the body is a temple, but it is so readily misused and abused through lack of discipline, overwork, overeating and many other things to excess … or the complete opposite as neglect. When you're young, it might seem quite easy to 'burn the candle at both ends', but as one gets older bones, the cells, and organs within you are weaker, and more susceptible to wear and tear.

This is bound to impact your decisions of why, how, and even where you live. So, many types of nourishment for the body have a massive effect upon you throughout your whole life. It might seem strange, but this affects you even beyond life.

Over the years, I have spoken on numerous occasions regarding the importance of nature, with its goodness and sustaining properties, and food is obviously one of these. Therefore, I ask you, what type of food do you usually eat? Do you think you eat healthily and/or in moderation?

Acknowledge and comprehend, as with any food or cocktail of ingredients, they can be harmful if taken to excess, but the consumption of 'simple' foods—for example fruit and nut—is highly beneficial, as they have a direct link to one's spiritual thoughts and process.

Farfetched to some, this may seem, but the goodness contained reflects the same upon the mind. Whereas the overeating of spicy/hot foods should be minimal, for they not only fuel the flames of thirst but also ignite the fires of the mind too. I will not dictate or ever decree whether one should eat 'flesh', other than you should live through your own conscience. Once again, from my heart, I ask only for you to always love the things that you think … cannot think.

This now leads me to the 'mind' and how it continually needs stimulation. It seeks fulfilment from the senses, which can have a positive or negative impact not only upon the body, but also your soul. Perhaps you may first think of your mind as being separate from one another's, but how can you say for sure? How many times have you heard or said to someone, "I knew what you were thinking" or "what you were going to say."

The body, mind, and soul (as we have covered previously) are all connected to each other by lines of communication, though there are no fibre optic cables transmitting pre-destined 'programs' for you to observe or digest. Love is energy. So, try to ensure it is love which transmutes and transmits the frequencies and impulses to do what you say, think, feel, or do.

Because love is universal and is all creation, then the consciousness of the mind is one. That said, I embed certain barriers or filters into 'you', to only receive what (and when) you are capable of. Remember, you can only learn to the level that you have reached.

Picture a coffee machine. It has a filter which strains the coffee beans and water, which lets you enjoy a cleaner, fresher, and purer drink. Likewise, the mind, because of an individual's 'capacity', also requires the same in terms of its experience and knowledge. They are inevitably linked. One leads to the other. Appreciate then, that if the mind was continually open to all frequencies and many energies, it would cease to function, exploding from just another form of 'excess'.

Those who have become 'mentally' ill, or what most call mentally 'disabled', may somehow seem disadvantaged to the onlooker, stranger, or even a family member. Remember, though, you are all perfect to me. The current sojourn (or soul journey) embarked upon has its reasons and purpose, which can be far more detailed than one can even begin to imagine.

Just as important to comprehend is that, during these many lessons, I have often stated about the fickleness of the mind and how easily it can lead to indecision and give rise to inner and outer conflict. This is because inner stresses can lead to disease (dis-ease) and one's own bodily pain. They also inflict pain outwardly upon others—usually those you love—through anger, fear, and hatred, in conjunction with an ego which is intolerant and lacks control.

In great contrast, when light has entered your heart—through compassion, forgiveness, and humility—it enriches you both inside and out. This transforms into the energy of love, which emanates through and from the mind. And those create waves of truth, positive in design. In fact, they radiate, spiralling through your own consciousness, into the ether and across time and space.

Remember, as you sow, so shall you reap. Hence, the same is reflected ... both through and to your soul. Illumination of the true 'you' is therefore defined not only by what you say and do, but also by what you think. So, the soul—just like the body and mind—needs sustenance to be fulfilled.

Overall, this is an easier process for the body. It can consume food (or water) slowly or rapidly, though can still become bloated. Similarly, for the mind, as it can digest many works of literature and information yet could equally seem to diminish with a lack of enthusiasm, commitment, or a loss of will.

Meanwhile, the soul's radiance and brilliance are totally dependent. Not by what you bring to the 'table', but in what you share from your heart, freely and with truth and sincerity. In turn, this helps sustain other souls, both near and far. As always, your life is yours to live. Ultimately, the responsibility for peace and harmony to sustain the human race is truly each your own. Amen.

LESSON 42:
SERENITY

When you walk the path of truth, please understand that your life will become serene and full of contentment. Of this, there can be no doubt. One only needs to ask whether they are feeling this way right now, and if you're not, then why not?

Each of your soul journeys (sojourns) upon the 'earth-plane' are milestones, though some may say millstones. This is because of the burden of imbalance, karma, and one's life's tasks … not only to those around you, like neighbours, friends, or family, but also unto yourself. Do you sense such weight upon your shoulders? Do you think or believe you need to escape or actually embrace such trials and tribulations?

Well, know my responsibilities are no less. You are each a part of me—being my 'children' of light—yet you could also envisage me as your father, mother, brother, sister, uncle, aunt, a grandparent, niece, nephew, and son, and so forth.

However, the mind can only attempt and try to portray me, somehow picturing me with a name, to place me in a pigeonhole, or describe me as some sort of physical being. So, whether you feel that 'I am I', the God within, the Great 'White' Spirit, an ethereal deity, pure Atma, or a supreme entity, they are all but names for who, where, and what we all are, which is love.

As we have recently discussed, if, or when, you need additional sustenance, thinking that your life is stressful or has become overbearing, getting in touch with the 'love' within—and around you—becomes of greater importance. In such times, I always ask you to become 'still', turning your 'thoughts' to off. When you sit in silence, you can hear me and the truth, but I realise, of course, this is not always possible. Therefore, I now ask you to come for a walk.

Take yourself to the woods or a forest if you can. But once again, if this is not feasible, then use the mind properly and let it take you swiftly there … to a place of peace, beauty, and true serenity. Why not imagine yourself there right now - there you go, it is as easy as ABC, isn't it! Now let's go for a walk together.

In front of you is a great and ancient woodland, with its trees so high …

they appear to touch the sky. You also notice there is not an entrance to this splendour, because any fence or boundary which attempts to trick you is an illusion. Understand, too, that you are not trespassing. So, never feel you're an unworthy soul who should not be here to experience and grow within the light.

There is a pathway now before you. Gladly accept and follow it. As you do, your footsteps remain upon smooth and untroubled ground, as leaves and pine needles form a natural layer of protection, enabling you to keep right on track. You are without fear of harm or injury. Here, your trust strengthens you.

All around you is the proof of everlasting life, isn't that what you wanted to see and hear? Yes indeed, even-aged trees must eventually wither and fall but, as they do, new life emerges from the decomposing bark and branches. Here, the insects and small creatures thrive upon its 'body', sustaining their own growth for the many days, weeks, months, and years to come.

Then, in the space now revealed, new seeds will rest there, carried by my breath, to continue the cycle of death and rebirth. You, though, having a conscience and free-will, could choose a new and brighter way. This leads to eternal life through peace and bliss.

Self-realization brings you to me ... and vice versa, me to you. Not because we have travelled over great distances to meet, but because it clears up that fog of confusion which has been built up, just like a wall between us. But this is fake. It is unreal and not solid. Hence your outstretched and loving arms reach through and embrace me, and you'll know it is yourself which has seemed to hide upon the 'other 'side.'

You now notice the evergreen trees standing tall on either side of the path. They are ever present, and remain so strong, once again protecting you from harmful gales or from those angry words whipped up just like a storm ... attempting to shift your equanimity. You know that these so-called 'good and bad' times are not meant to lure or deviate you away from your course. They are to help instil an unshakable faith within you ... through 'experience'.

So, as you travel further into the depths, one could forgive you in thinking the deeper the trail—or you could read this as trial—it becomes ... you imagine it as one of darkness and fear, but this is not the case. Please, just look up and see.

Above you, a canopy of tree-tops and branches protect you from sudden rainfall, like those unexpected tears when your heart suffers through emotional, mental, spiritual, or physical pain. Yet it still lets in the light of the sun—and Son—because those rays pierce through, similar to a hot knife in butter. This is the hope you can rely upon. It is never ending, constantly guiding, and will never abandon you.

Now, as you pause for a moment to look towards the light, a ray shines through and brings great warmth to your face. You feel so much more 'alive'. While you bask within it, your heart is lifted, knowing you need—or that you actually depend—upon 'it'. Likewise, so does the source of truth, for like a mirror, you are all a reflection of me.

The intensity and brightness force you to close your eyes. It fills your mind full of colour. Vivid red, vibrant orange and brilliant yellow all form an image of a new horizon. You seem lost within the moment. Such beauty is wondrous, with a feeling of tranquillity and oneness.

It is precisely this which helps you to appreciate you are never alone, and hence, should never feel 'lonely'. Unlike fair-weather friends who come and go during the 'good' times in your life, I am your true rest and refuge. I am your fortitude and your strength, so I will guide you through the thick and thin, helping you to clear imbalance and any 'sin'.

Continue to move now, and do not stop 'til the battle is won.' Your task, your pathway may be straight and narrow, or it may lead you on multiple detours and routes of sacrifice or pleasure and pain ... but know this; I am with you every step of the way. No one—or nothing—can distract me from you, or from this course. So, keep looking up. Let the shadows of the past fall behind you, so your unseen future becomes but a glimpse of the serenity to follow.

So then, your discovery in that the earthly road is temporary and will now remind you your true path is eternal ... with your current journey bringing you full circle, only to find your true self. Amen.

LESSON 43:
ELEVATED

Be still thy soul and come to me with an open heart. Know that my arms are forever outstretched towards you. I welcome and embrace your light, which shines so brightly amongst the darkness ... where doubt and fear attempt to smother and hide the truth.

We are 'one', dear child. You were not born but are a spark of divinity, emerging from before the beginning of time. It was my will., and so it came to pass for all life, in every space and dimension. Therefore, no matter what their shape or appearance, every living thing retains the light. It has its purpose to fulfil and complete.

Like a leaf floating upon a gentle breeze, it will rest precisely where it is meant to. So do you, as the soul ... whether that is within the body of your current incarnation where it lives, or by continuing its natural growth upon the immeasurable planes of vibration and ether. Some may now feel that this is all a dream—a kind of 'dreamland'—or that it is all a whimsical notion or thought of a dreamer. But it is all fact and not fiction.

Some days, when you are bombarded by images of anger, hatred, disease, or war across the television screen, or upon hearing of such things on the radio—perhaps even reading about atrocities in the newspapers—it can all become too easy to despair. Hence the uttering of words of anguish or sorrow, be that for a child, man, woman, or even for nature. Know that it is precisely these times when you must look through and from the heart. Understand there is always - yes, always - a glimmer of hope.

I see many tears which fall, from those bearing witness to the images of those trying to sleep ... not within a bed, but on the streets. The same when a child begs for food, stomach bloated from malnutrition. Or, for the animal dying of thirst, ignored by passers-by, or worse still, its so-called 'master' ... who is, in reality, a master of none.

Therefore, to help you all, I often cast uplifting words towards and through you, but I state these things today for two very good reasons. First, to repeat that you do not fear when I am near. Second, to remind you of being grateful for all that you are, all that you have and all that you can become.

In times of uncertainty—in what seems to an unforgiving world—change your mindset and just believe. Yes, believe in the goodness that lies within you and in all things. Reach for it. Then share it, sending positive thoughts, prayers, and words of hope to those in need. Even more important is to let your hands do the work of love, to aid, support and guide those who are less fortunate than yourself. Remember, hands that do are holier than lips that pray.

If you feel that any burden is too much to bear, understand that I forever watch over you. All you need to do is to ask me to help you in truth; for it is only in truth that the answers—and the right course of action unfold—for whatever is your highest good. Likewise, for the higher good of those close by and also who seem so very far away too. Trust me, and trust in yourself. That is all that you need to do.

Comprehend that when you are still and at peace, you feel my presence, away from the clutter within the mind and that which envelops the body. I wrap you in my love. This is my gift, my present ... pre-sent during the eternal dawn of awakening. Be soothed now by gentle lullabies and the sound of two hearts beating as one. I empower you with all that I am, so that you can truly realise and become what you are destined to be ... your 'true self'.

In reality, you can elevate beyond the false image of what you currently may think of as 'you'. You will appreciate—and finally know that you are life in its truest form, which is 'light'. Now, as you resonate through and upon higher frequencies, new understanding will flow like water over rock, cascading from energy points around your soul through many chakras ... which can stabilize your very being. New knowledge will bring and provide you with the wisdom, through living the experience of 'man' and so much more ... so very much more.

As I am I, realise I am all ... and everything is all I am. Then each one of you can move further and grow far beyond what may seem mere words. Of these, and other such texts throughout history, they serve their purpose. Messages which one can simply place within a bottle and let it float, drifting upon the ocean of truth, or you can digest and intake what touches you deep inside to never hide again.

So, do you now recognize the love inside you? Can you feel my love around you, protecting you, supporting you, and encouraging you to know thyself, too? Because, when you have realised who, what, and why you 'are', then you will see with new clarity, having the clearer vision of and from and through the heart. The illusion of separateness and the fog of forgetfulness will dissipate and fade away. On the horizon, another path of your journey will lie before you.

This time you will know where you have been, and more importantly, where you are ... for the crown of my heart beckons and will never forget you. Each of your souls are the jewels scattered throughout creation. You are all finding your way home through the 'experience' you have chosen or need to complete ... hence are inevitably linked, too.

May all beings and all 'life' not let those tears of pain or so-called injustices ever tarnish this truth, because not one soul shall pass me by. So too, not a single tear will fade or disappear, for they are precious beyond compare. Therefore, I catch every single one.

As I have stated before, they hang in suspension around me, connected by cords of light ... reminding, helping, nurturing all both within and out. They too shine eternal, like diamonds and stars, which magnify right from wrong, love from hate and peace from war. And the truth illuminates from the biggest lie of all ... that death of the body is the end. Amen.

LESSON 44:
WAITING?

By now, you realise I live within, without, above, and below you. There isn't any place I cannot be. You also understand that distance—or any dimension—can never delay my presence, for I am all things, everywhere and within everything, since time immemorial.

Even so, there are still those who choose not to believe in their own divinity, and therefore in me. They prefer to view theories of evolution. For example ... the perquisite to the human species' presence upon the Earth. I will never condemn or belittle such viewpoints, but state that it is only through having an open heart that one can attempt to experience such a great potential of life and energy ... beyond the body and mind.

As these both resonate upon a denser and much slower rate of vibration, they inhibit and can also restrict higher frequencies from piercing through the ether towards your higher self, your consciousness, and soul.

One can easily envisage wearing a woolly hat upon a cold day, a desire to keep your head warm, and to protect you against the elements. However, without pursuing wisdom from and through the heart, the 'hat' (like the exposed mind) merely becomes an invisible shield or barrier—to you, that is—which insulates your whole being from actually experiencing true joy and inner peace. This is quite bizarre; would you not agree?

This occurs not because you are specifically trying to prevent your spark of divinity from igniting into a higher and brighter flame of light, but it is because one does precisely the opposite, which is to do nothing! Or one may become even more attached to the physical and its 'needs', removing one's focus ... 'taking your eyes off the ball' one might say.

So, is there a secret still to be discovered? Perhaps some sort of magical potion could miraculously remove any impediments ... that stifle the immense power within you? Or could you actually be waiting for the second coming of the Messiah, before you can contemplate something far greater than what you currently think you are?

Interestingly, if you can reconsider the word Messiah and then replace it with a messenger, then you would immediately recognize that he has never left you at all. This is because he shines in every heart, but not all bear witness to the innate goodness within. If they did, then they would know and understand what true happiness actually is.

Remember, Jesus was, is, and always will be a great healer of humanity. So too, have the many saints, guru's and avatars spoken 'truth', often to no avail … but understand the world is no longer in a permanent slumber. Many souls have risen to radiate and share their love across the world at this time, just like a call to arms.

Please appreciate, though, this is not a battle fought over foreign lands or across seas, where death, pain, and misery become inflicted upon man, woman, child, animal, and all of nature. No, it is with open hands, outstretched to welcome the change from the old to the new 'you', and one which must be fought with endeavour and fortitude, lest your determination wanes and perseverance falters.

As I have said before, there needs no special date to pass, such as a New Year for resolutions to be made. These often slip away, falling by the wayside unless immediate 'results' are gained. Therefore, days, dates, and timing are irrelevant in the grand scheme of things. An hour on one planet could last weeks, months, or even years upon another. The only decision you need to make is to actually start to be the true you.

Mmm … now I hear countless thoughts such as, "But what if I like me the way I am?" Ok, well, that's intriguing. Though perhaps they could all answer this: you are indeed perfection in your heart and soul … but what about in what you say, think, and do? Can you state there is never any room for improvement? So, understand, if you had nothing to learn, nothing else to do or experience, and if no 'joy' was to come from your presence upon the 'earth-plane', then why are you there?

You have at your disposal an armoury which can defeat your one true enemy, which is yourself. Such demons as doubt and fear, attachment and desire, and anger and hate can all be dispelled and conquered with the shield of faith. This is as large and wide as you need it to be. With it, you can protect others as well as yourself; and yet, this is only another choice to be made.

Likewise, with the well of hope, you can quench your own thirst to instil an unwavering attitude and demeanour. But you can also pour forth the same to someone less fortunate, whose need may be far greater (if you look through your heart) than your own.

So now the wait is over. It is time to pick up the sword of truth and march forward into your destiny. The ego must be slain. Yes, cut into two. Therefore, compassion and forgiveness not only shine forth but also stay behind, living within those memories and hearts where you have been. Those footsteps will not fade and disappear as if walking upon sand. Instead, they will leave an eternal trace, becoming examples of how-to walk-in truth for countless souls to follow.

You can read—and re-read—this message and lesson as many times as it needs to be. Allow it to sink within, deep inside your core. This will stir you into 'right' action because karma is not just for one heart and soul, but for the many.

I encourage and bless you as I offer thee, my grace. May this be the additional strength as and when you require it, upon your continuing journey. Comprehend and know it is abundant, never ending and all sustaining. So, please, look for and feel it wherever you may be. Amen.

LESSON 45:

BLESSED

One by one, the days of your life continue to roll by. You, as the inquirer, the aspirant or devotee can now pause for thought. Perhaps you'll wonder how far you have come during the past year.

Maybe you'll be considering what life's 'lessons' you have learned, mulling over those decisions and choices you had made within situations of (or over) work, friends and family? You might even recall those actions which caused regret, those so-called mistakes which irritated the mind and heart ... and no amount of wishful thinking can change them.

Yes indeed, every single one of your thoughts, prayers, actions, deeds, and words forms a network of joy or agony. Like the veins within the body —and your spiralling DNA—these are all connected. The results of them all flow like blood to the heart. They either nourish or emanate light, or they carry the sadness of pain and shadow.

As this passage of time, which you call the 'year', slowly draws to a close ... only a few weeks remain. The Christmas 'period' can begin. Trees will be erected in countless homes ... decorations will be hung, cards posted, and phone calls made, all of which form part of the annual reminder of the birth of Christ.

These should be days of joy for the world. And no matter what faith or religion in which you believe or follow, peace should reign. Hope and love ought to resonate and echo within every heart and home, too. Contentment for, and of, who and what you are, can then elevate you all above doubt and fear. This enables humanity to connect through body, mind, and spirit ... but will it?

In these hectic moments, many areas of one's life can attempt to divert and side-track you away from the truth and me. The commercial pressure, with materialism and the expenditure of money, brings both stress and disease to the mind and the household. Yet for some, there aren't such choices. They don't have worries over which party clothes to wear, as they just simply wish to find somewhere to sleep or some food to eat.

Understand please, this 'lesson will not turn into (and what some may call) a guilt trip. Nor relayed to you in the desire to make you feel any different from what you already do, that's unless you wish to. Only you can determine change within or without the 'self.' No amount of persuasion can alter that, just like someone who sees obstructions to a diet, getting fit, or becoming educated through additional training. Remember, 'you can lead a horse to water but you cannot make it drink.'

Realise too, around the world, conflict, malnutrition, anger, hate, and fear cross continents like an airborne virus. Only by utilizing the filters of non-discrimination, compassion, and discernment can you all make the correct choices and decisions to transfer and dilute such negativity. This will bring a new calmness to humanity and Mother Earth.

So then, having woken upon this new day, are you grateful for your sleep, whilst having the ability to even rise from your bed? When you opened your eyes, is there gratitude for seeing the alarm clock, while there are others who have no sight. Then, as you dress, putting on extra clothes for warmth upon a cold winter's day, can you spare a thought for those who walk half naked on their own road and journey of experience? When you wash your face and clean your teeth with clean water—perhaps leaving the tap running—does a notion trickle down from the mind and into your heart ... for those who pray for just a single sip to quench their thirst?

Don't be sad. Please comprehend that love is stronger than all other things, and so it will prevail, though you must want it to. Can you? Now consider the Christmas dinner table this year. Will you be grateful for the luxury of choice and the food to eat, be it savoury or sweet? Would you know if a friend, neighbour, or even a stranger in the same street (or across the world) goes without, or eats scraps to survive? Yes indeed, while 80% of the world thrives, are the rest denied, with tears ... asking how and why?

Do you feel blessed to have the love of a friend, a father, mother, sister, brother, or even a loyal and beloved pet? Appreciate also, there are those who sit or walk seemingly alone, feeling neglected by kith and kin, by society, the state or country, and even the world.

For those I speak of, I say and tell you ... I walk with every step you take. And know this ... I hold your hands while I place your hearts within my own. I cradle you within my grace, of which I pour over your souls to eternally sustain you. Whilst you may often feel the world has abandoned you, realise you are not—and never can be—a stranger to me, as we are forever 'one'.

Those without a bed, whether through one's own karma and experience, shall lie down in my fields of peace. The fragrance of my divine essence will lift thy heart to magical planes ... beyond the fear and dread of the night and cold. The emptiness of belly, please understand, is only temporary. I will fulfil you within and out by sitting at my table—within the Kingdom of Heaven—nourished by trust, belief, and an unwavering faith.

Right now, may every one of you count your blessing this Christmas time. Be grateful for whatever mercy is placed there for you. Do not doubt yourself to become even brighter next year, to shine and share the truth within. May you become the true you for all those you encounter upon the Earth … whether that's in your own thoughts, through spoken word, or even upon the ether in your dreams whist you sleep. Blessed be, Amen.

LESSON 46:
KEEPER

Welcome to our connection, as always. Try not to feel saddened or even overjoyed by my words, and those feelings which flow through (or wash over) you as you read or hear them. Rather, treat them with equanimity. Balance will be quickly restored to your energy, both within and out. It will enable you to move forward on an even keel. Therefore, even if another's hope fades, you will be the strength someone—or the many—need or wishes for.

Taking each day at a time will be the best approach as you make your way through this life. It will help you embrace trials, tribulations, situations, and people with a single-mindedness ... to do, be, say, and think of truth and righteousness. Then, as you continue on your road and journey, know that 'giving' (of yourself) can be the true sacrifice, because you provide others with the most precious thing you have, which is love ... your divine love.

More often than not, you'll find it has been easier for you to keep it, unknowingly becoming frightened to share the essence of what you are. Maybe it is fear (or in feeling vulnerable) if you wear your heart upon your sleeve in case it is crushed or swept aside ... accidentally or purposefully, by another who crosses your soul-journey/sojourn upon the 'earth-plane' at this time.

I urge you to display and let your kindness; generosity; compassion, and thoughtfulness pour out from the well of your heart. Do not become the keeper who hides this richness and splendour within. If that was the case, those who draw close to you cannot see the real you. This is like attempting to lower a bucket into your pool of love, only to find it has been covered.

Without this flow, not only does the bucket—this hand of friendship and hope—feel dry and empty, but in not 'giving', the well is hindered, struggling to be replenished from the fountain which runs from me to you. It becomes stagnant and full of imbalance with those minute particles of self-inflicted denial, negativity, unhappiness, and fear. Therefore, please use your instinct, your intuition ... and all the while try to listen to your conscience, which is 'I', prompting you when indecision strikes.

Like the elephants of the African plains, they know precisely where to roam and travel to find the source of water which sustains them. So do you, if you only open your heart. You can do this permanently, and, as I have stated many times, the well of my heart will never run dry, for every one of you may quench your thirst in me.

I am limitless. I will not be a 'keeper', refusing or denying you what you seek. And I am not your 'only for tomorrow' God, either. Ultimately, through self-realization, you will understand this is the very same 'within'. Just believe it for it to become true. Then the same can manifest and pour forth like water over rock, eroding ego and disdain for your fellow man.

Do not concern yourself with the speed of the 'flow' at this stage. You can only learn to the level you have reached. But appreciate that deep ingrained karmic imbalance is reduced and eventually disappears under the pressure of truth and love. Negativity will drain away. Like a sieve, I will filter the impediments and irritations of desire, greed, anger, and jealousy to leave those golden nuggets of your character and personality, to shine forth like a beacon for others to see and bear witness to. Indeed, they will also radiate—shining the light from within and their own higher 'self' too—which attracts others to know and feel the same.

Understand, please, while upon the world, all that glitters is not gold. Though what I speak of here today is unmistakable, for it cannot be tarnished, scratched, or even worn on the physical. No, these words sparkle and illuminate throughout the ether like stars, because they depict the true 'you'… and your development as a soul and being of light.

Perhaps … you could re-ask yourself one day, "Who am I?" just like the 'lesson' in Book 1. Then, as, and when it is time for your physical overcoat —called the body—to be discarded, your soul will feel it has fulfilled its purpose, and served you well so you could serve others, too. No one could ever wish to think differently about their loss of mortality, while passing into their true reality, could they?

Remember too, regarding your feelings and the attachment to your so-called possessions and all things within the permanent world, for you cannot keep them with you. All are merely 'trinkets' and irrelevant in the grander scheme of things. Only your heart and all love contained there goes on.

You may work your fingers to the bone and accumulate property, money, and all manner of luxuries, but as mentioned before, they can help you live, but they cannot teach or show you how to live. 'Class' comes not from ownership or upon the standard of your journey, but from what you do and complete within it. Always keep this in mind.

Understand too, within this modern age in which you live, it is very difficult to steer away from attitudes and those ingrained beliefs of 'what is yours and of what is mine'. This often stems from the media and society in general, but you must. You are not a sheep of 'man', but form part of my flock, which I never lose sight of. Newspapers, radio, and, worst of all, the 'tell-lie-vision' ... create desire, knowingly or unknowingly feeding lower based vibration and energy to rise, which only causes confusion and illusion to the masses.

But you now know the truth. You can see it with a clearer vision and one mindedness. We are not divided or separated. We are inevitably linked; for you are all like droplets of rain, and after what seems a short or long journey (to you) will merge once more into the ocean of my love. Realise you are safe, eternally within the shores of my loving arms, a harbour of rest and peace. I am the keeper of your life, your hopes, your dreams, and this is the reality of your heart and soul forever. Amen.

LESSON 47:
THE RETURN

Deep within—for so many of you—there's still such burning questions as 'Why am I here?', 'Where am I going?' and 'Is there a Heaven?' And, though the mind has learned and digested much information, the soul aches for confirmation and for some 'hard' evidence of our 'oneness' and 'me'.

One may also look upon many of these lessons, where I have talked about the 'journey' you have embarked and travel upon throughout this lifetime, and by considering these, help and lead you to your own self-realization of whom and what you are. Because of this, one will eventually change their perception ... through knowing the truth.

You will no longer think of a destination but understand the true purpose of the 'experience' (of your life). Hence, you can come to terms with not concerning yourself in what you think or believe will materialize at the end of your sojourn—soul journey—but of what you have achieved ... and how far you have come as a soul and as a human being.

In fact, if you could observe yourself, you would see so much angst, seriousness, stress, and pain of this 'process.' This is nearly all unnecessary. In doing so, appreciate you can be your own worst enemy, by having ill-thoughts, words, and deeds. Know then that these hinder and slow down one's development and the ability for growth and illumination. Your love can become stifled and withdrawn, reflecting your own doubt and misapprehension of the connection with your fellow man.

So, by taking time out, from the hustle and bustle of your daily tasks to contemplate and become 'still', you find that the pause for breath can be an elixir of life. With the mind turned to 'off', and disengaged from self-induced worry, your heart can open to feel my love within and around you. Therefore, a restless spirit becomes a restful one.

You'll no longer feel as if you're in a bubble, seemingly alone and separated from me or from those you love. The wafer-thin barrier of illusion can be simply burst. Like a cocoon, you can shed your 'thick' skin—or ego—to reveal a softer and more attentive, compassionate 'you'. This does not make one weak. In fact, it strengthens you. The transition from the belief of (and in) your own physicality has blossomed into spirituality.

In its recognition, you can take flight beyond such dense energy and low vibrations to elevate further and higher into the light. Your divine essence can radiate, and thus bloom like a beautiful flower bathed in the eternal sunshine of my heart.

It would be very easy indeed, to then assume you now have made a return, somehow coming back to me from where you came. However, this is untrue. You have never, ever left me, even though what you currently go through seems to show you have.

Some may feel that it all seems like a game, this physicality of your body, as you work, rest and play. That said, isn't all theatre a pantomime? Am I the puppeteer who casts some unfavourably, whilst placing others in prominent positions upon a stage called life? Remember, I am the 'do-er' within you. Yes, it's true, but I do not control you as you have the free-will which is, (and gives you), 'choice'.

I only enact and carry out through you the truth … the whole truth, and nothing but the truth. It is you as a soul who, through karma—movement/action—achieves and transcends balance and imbalance to others and of what reflects unto yourself. Because this is so, you become your very own judge and jury, judging everything that has ever occurred. Therefore, no secrets can ever be kept away from 'Universal' justice. It is not I who stands upon a pedestal … who meets out so-called just rewards or suffering, even though millions of you think I do.

I re-state these things, not to make you feel any additional pressure—as you can already do or make these seem this way yourself—but to simplify such issues. You all need to realise and understand love is simple, and life is simply love. All life upon the world would interact and be sustained if this was just taken on board in one's thought processes and actions. So, can you? Could you?

This voyage of discovery has not left the dock. It does not need to reach a new port, as you have always been upon the ocean of my love. I am not the stowaway—deep inside you—who does not wish to be found or even ignored … but I am I, the Indweller of your heart, who can help you at all times and in all places. Know that I am not a captain who barks orders to make you comply, trying to control you either.

If you let—or even command—me, like a sail upon a mast, or a ship's wheel or rudder, my aim is to guide, lead, encourage, and support you in every endeavour. As we are 'one,' I can do this for you …just by realising that you are the vessel, and that I am the true power of your magnificence. Then, by keeping faith in yourself, you'll have the belief. And by having this belief, you will trust not only in me, but of those actions deemed (but not always are), your own.

Please try to never sink into your own demise of fear or neglect. Those who you have become emotionally 'attached' to can be affected physically by such negativity and pain. Like a whirlpool, do not become too close or ever get trapped within the circles of deceit, for they not only confuse and abuse. Such elements can spread out of control, disorientating the heart and soul.

In these circumstances, it is only love which can break you free. It will pull you up into safer—and calmer—emotional waters, to continue peacefully once more. Eventually, a new dawn will rise upon and in your mind. It is then, and only then, you will truly believe you have not 'returned'. In fact, you have been nowhere else, other than within my loving arms and inside my heart. Amen.

LESSON 48:
FOCUS

Welcome once again, in the knowledge our connection is as strong as ever, no matter what transpires or materializes around you. Even though circumstances and situations may seem to detract or divert us, this is only but a thought or notion, which is unsustainable. Therefore, if—or when—calamity, chaos, or mayhem peruses, surrounds, or ensnares you … only by being true to self can you regain the focus required to move forward and leave such things as discrimination behind you.

What I speak of can range from what is physically around you, and all that is dense within the impermanent world. Also, the mental or emotional disturbances within your mind and heart because they are inevitably linked.

First, we could look at the impermanent world and how it can create disease/disharmony amongst you. Some may think of the 'material' as being solid, such as concrete, wood, steel, but what seems like structure is just appearance. In fact, as I have previously mentioned … everything is energy, atoms, molecules, and such like. As this is so, they are all moving at different rates of vibration.

Your body is no different. Most of it comprises water, and so you, as a 'vessel' are also constantly moving. The soul also resonates, and when in peace and harmony, it moves so fast it can seem almost static in appearance, but the light within radiates immeasurably.

So, it is the denseness of the world which causes illusion. It attaches you to it through the senses. The desires of the material world tempt you. They try to keep love from the heart, equanimity from the mind and the light from the soul. A process which attempts to enslave you to constant emptiness, unfulfilled until your dying day. But living this way only leads to the search, whether it's for someone or something which can apparently fill—even temporarily—the void.

This is not on the exterior, but it is within you. So, how can you mind the gap? Well, imagine for a moment you are traveling on a train, which then stops at the side of a platform. You don't just open the doors and drop; you move to step over the space towards the safety of the ground. Even at nighttime, you may not see the drop, but you automatically alight the train this way, don't you? Indeed, you could argue it is with a basic leap of faith. It shows this in its simplest form and means by which to counteract doubt, from what can seem a perilous drop below.

So then, why do you have these senses? How can you use them and focus on the truth? Well, firstly imagine a clear container with ten holes, and let's now call it your body. No matter how much light passes through it, some will always escape before it can be seen for what it truly is.

Therefore, the senses are an opportunity to help you learn and control desire, and also the mind, body, and soul. By understanding this, you can—through experience—prevent the leakage of whom and what you are. Only then is your true clarity of vision restored. You can illuminate and shine the light as a spark of divinity, as you will have regained your focus.

Now, if you look back upon your life, can you think of when you have succumbed to 'desire' and a lack of contentment? Perhaps this was in a relationship, or for physical items such as a home, a car, or T.V and such like. Or was it for a dream, a hope, and a wish which then turned into an all-consuming passion. These can be commendable, but can also dissolve trust, eradicate friendship, and even break a marriage, which is the ultimate exercise in controlling your senses.

One can also consider here that the desire for greater strength within the body, mind, and heart is a positive note. When you have physical, mental, and spiritual 'strength', then you really can do 'service' in the true sense of the word. So, try to remember this in order: food, head, and God.

As the days, weeks, months, and years go by, faster as you age, do you continue as you are (some may say aimlessly), or actively pursue the goal in sight? Will you let your future drift by and fade like a New Year's resolution, or can you recognize the power of change within you?

Everyone has a choice; you all have a choice. You only need to decide what to do with the time and the life that you have chosen and been given. Of course, you can never turn the clock back. But each moment in truth shines eternal and can therefore bring you closer to the person and soul inside which you long to be.

Within every heart, one's goodwill, generosity, kindness, and peace can light up and blaze a glorious pathway ahead. Not only will this help you iron out the peaks and the troughs and any trials and tribulations of the journey, but those who are also working or living on different levels of energy and vibration or dimensions. How cool is that?

As stated, many times before, we are all inevitably linked upon a golden chain which unites and never divides. It is not made of so-called precious metals, but formed by light, through and from, and into my heart. As we are one, I also hallmarked you with purity… and only the cast of illusion, like a shell, encases you.

I AM I The Indweller of Your Heart—Book Three

I ask you then to focus upon the love that is you. This brings your attention and focus to me. You'll recognize only the reflection, but it is within a mirror which cannot distort or blur the true image and creation of me. Remember, I am with you always and forever … so just be true; and be you. Amen.

LESSON 49:
TIME

Live in the moment! I start this lesson with a statement, not only to make you think and ponder (when you can pause from what you call 'living'), but also because—as your eternal witness—I can see if you can enact upon it in your work, rest, and play.

So, as I have mentioned many times before, each of you speaks of those months and years which roll by seamlessly, one after the other. Then, before you know it, periods of your earthbound existence can (or will) simply become phases of experience which can blur and fade. Or they can stand out from the crowd, so prominently, because of whom and what you are and have achieved.

For others, whether it is within childhood and teenage years, which leads to adulthood, and then retirement, these may well be looked upon as time wasted, possibly with deep regret. These emotions may surface by becoming someone who had the wish, but not the desire, to fulfil one's potential as a soul and human being. As such, understand that time is irrelevant in the grander scheme of things.

Many will say it gives you structure, and without the hands of a clock, you could not survive and live. But are the seconds, minutes, and hours the true pillars of your existence? Can 'time' really be this important and significant? Is this a way to guide you upon your path and sojourn, into the dense and physical energy of the 'earth-plane?'

Let's consider an egg-timer. Now visualize turning it upside down and waiting. As the grains of sand slip by, forming an empty side of the vessel, the passing of time has taken place. You yourself were the witness. So, do you sense or feel any different now? If not, why is this? Have you seen this as a waste of your important 'time'? Do you ever become emotional about it? Please appreciate that it is not about how little or how much of your time you have, but what you do with it that counts.

Right now, if you had only a minute to live, what would you think, say, or do? Remember, it is only love which lasts, as it leaves a legacy across, through, to, and from you. Therefore, all of your thoughts, words, and deeds can either ignite the fire—which continues to support the spark of your own divine essence—or this source of such power beyond your imagination can literally become void of emotion. It will appear empty, just like one half of the egg-timer.

But once again, is this really true? Know that a vacuum can contain 'life', even if minute particles or elements seem to have disappeared. The problem with this notion is most of humankind still thinks two dimensionally. I have explained before, you do not need to look outside the box, because no 'box' actually exists.

So then, how can you become emotionally unattached to time, and yet remain balanced, strong, and true every day? Perhaps you could firstly reconsider the first line of this lesson and live in the moment. To do this only takes you to be yourself—your true 'self'—and not what any other person, any being or indeed any 'thing' wishes you to be … or wants to see.

How easily this can be is also down to you, the so-called individual. For example, you can surely remember at least one instance when you were somewhere you didn't want to be. All the while, deep inside, wishing yourself away. What were you trying to do and achieve? Was it to please someone else? It is important to understand I am not suggesting anyone be selfish or arrogant in their actions. Nor should they hurt any other soul or being, but merely ask you to recognize the feelings inside of you.

Please comprehend that your emotions are the key to unlocking time itself. Therefore, how you feel within your heart can transcend age, distance, space, and every dimension. A loved one, whether they are still 'living' or if they have crossed over, (having removed their physical overcoat/body) can be as near and dear to you either way.

Realise too, those who you state are in 'Spirit', do not even contemplate time as important or relevant in their own development and growth as a soul, because there isn't any need for it. Only in the connections made upon the world, where you all place dates and times to schedule 'life'—just like a diary—can this become an issue.

Communication through the mental, physical, and spiritual realms isn't restricted at all, not by me. However, because love is truth, every spark of light will only—through their true divinity, which lies inherently within—act for the higher good (and on behalf) of the recipient. This is not the same as one who feels they are being ignored (through what seems a loss or fear). For instance, because a loved one has not appeared to them in a dream. Or not having sent a subliminal message across the ether and through the veil of so-called death.

Even if these things happen, such as feathers appearing, a smell of a fragrance, the feeling of a touch or helping hand, hearing a favourite song just at the right moment, and perhaps even a whisper into the mind or ear, they are often missed because of immense grief and falling tears. All along, your loved ones are as close, if not closer to you … than when you once walked and talked together.

So please, appreciate it is time, and time alone, which seems to divide and not guide you. Hence, when in the grip of pain—and what may feel like being crushed and broken—for some, the seconds, minutes, hours and the days, will not seem to become the 'healer' they can be.

Only by detaching yourself from the luminous clock face, which attempts to wrap your heart (freezing you into the depths of the night), can the 'unreal' finally become real. When you truly live in the moment, the connection to me (and to all) can be more apparent than a full moon upon a cloudless night sky, or the brilliant sun which rises on a beautiful summer morning.

Indeed, as you see and sense them both, you know they exist. So, how can I be any different? Love is 'one'. It is everything. Therefore, do not let 'time' become a factor in any way, shape, or form. It cannot come between you and me, or your true self, and of course, your heart to all things. Amen.

LESSON 50:

PURIFICATION

Welcome once more to our connection ... so your heart, mind, and soul can learn and digest this information and guidance 'within'. Remember too, it will always be up to you whether you believe in what you read, sense, and feel is right or not. But if you have picked up this book, then surely, what it contains will resonate inside of you.

Please understand that the truth—in whatever capacity—may sometimes seem to hurt. We can deem this as necessary, in order one can progress along their own path and journey. Ultimately, in learning, speaking, and accepting what is true and correct can only be beneficial, not only to yourself, but for those who are close to you, walking beside you on the road to peace and bliss.

Remember, anything worth having is indeed worth the fight. And as it is yourself who you must do battle with, then you already have an advantage. How so? Well, just like everyone else, you have strengths and weaknesses. Though it is the weakness of your own mind which can and needs to be purified. This enables even greater understanding, and through one's knowledge and experience be able to ascend one day, permanently leaving the mortal coil behind.

Like dirty hands, any experience can carry bacteria or infection. It is the ego which pierces the mind and requires cleansing over and over again, so that little or no trace of it remains. By humbling the mind, the ability to serve will multiply at least by ten, and perhaps even by one hundredfold, because without selfish thoughts or deeds infiltrating the body, the little 'I' (your ego) is cut down, and selflessness reigns.

After this, so much becomes easier to accept and share. You can detach even your most coveted possessions from the pull of the heartstrings, which was a last-ditch attempt to hang onto the impermanent and unimportant physical 'things'. Few can sacrifice such. They cannot cope with what seems to be a loss of the material, without feeling withdrawn, guilty, or shameful, in the belief that part of what makes them 'them', has somehow disappeared. In truth, it is the opposite, because any release from 'attachment' in its multitude of ways and feelings is beneficial ... for both the well-being of the heart and the purification of the soul.

Now think of your own body instead. Imagine not being able to bathe or shower for a week or even a month. How do you think you would feel, not just on the outside but also 'within' if your hair was lank, greasy, unkempt, and if your clothes were smelly, your skin irritated, and you had dirty fingernails and so on and so forth? An unpleasant thought, indeed. But could you cope? If so, how would this impact your daily life, upon your well-being and others close by?

Then, "What about my soul?" you may well ask. Well, can you imagine what negativity, dirt, and grime—through misplaced anger, fear, stress, and disease—has been accumulated over many lifetimes of inaction and karmic imbalance? As I have discussed before, your light (your divine essence), which is a beautiful spark of my heart, has drifted through the eras of time. Like a comet, it has collected almost immovable particles of doubt, hate, and painful tears along its current journey. Realise they all cling like sticky black molasses, just like glue, trying to disguise the truth and real you.

But no longer can—or will—this continue. Love is greater and more powerful than such inequities. Know then that finally, once and for all, the opportunity has arrived to erase all attitudes and elements of misaligned character and personality from your core being. Your energy, through receiving and protecting the true way to live—with human values of non-violence, peace, and kindness—will increase its rate of vibration. This resembles a comet too but caught by the gravitational pull of a large planet, to be cast out like a slingshot and speeding up. Therefore, darkness and decay and negativity will fall away, having been burnt and eradicated by the very love that I am, and which also blooms in you.

Rightly or wrongly, you may question me about why you must learn and go through any sort of process and development. But one must appreciate that because you are part of me, the sum of all parts makes us whole. It was you who had wished to experience 'life' this way. Then gradually, over many millennia, your senses distracted you. Desire seemed to imprison you, away from your true self, who is me, but no longer!

In this lesson, I finally ask for you to comprehend it is not by drinking a magical potion or holy water, reading sacred texts, and visiting ancient temples or buildings which can do this for you. Remember, you are without beginning and without end. You are actually free. Freedom is in you. You are light, for light is in you. You are love, for love is in you.

Dismantle then, those barriers and obstacles which have been placed in and around your heart. Show the world who and what you are, as a true being and soul who shines and illuminates, bringing happiness and joy to all whom you meet.

Forget now the past. Your very own future emerges from this present day in which you walk, talk, and act. Thus, in letting each moment bring peace, even into the heart of just one other, you also help them onto their own purification, too. Amen.

LESSON 51:
PROPHECY

So, the world did not end today after all, did it? Therefore, with so many people still looking for answers, this Mayan prophecy can either be deemed inaccurate, or just plainly false in its interpretation and design. But who analysed such, and can any information (or system) really predict or show the future?

Throughout history, every soul, and being of course, has all been enthralled, captivated, and also feared death. They count the days, weeks, months, or years until a 'doomsday' or catastrophic event influences and changes the world forever. Concerns, thoughts, dreams, and visions of heavenly bodies colliding, attacks by aliens, or even creatures of the night have been written, or filmed within Hollywood 'blockbusters', all depicting invasions, death, and disease.

However, you do not need me to explain or discuss such events. Every one of you already know about world wars, so-called 'natural' disasters—which affect hundreds of thousands, if not millions of people, animals and insects—as well as man-made 'errors' within nuclear facilities upon the earth.

So, to, many countries throughout time, instead of being run for the people, have—by various heads of state, presidents, and dictators—just abused their positions. They inflict suffering, as well as confusion and illusion, upon the masses, and across neighbouring nations, too. However, because of the inner balance required by each soul, no matter what the tragedy, people can still pull together. They can unite behind the banner or flag of truth; not rolling over to fade and die. People will stand as one, to eventually overcome all physical, mental, and emotional pain.

Please truly understand that love is the only form of healing which can disperse and then eradicate hate. Through loving words, thoughts, and deeds, they can break the hardened shell of deceit to reveal the truth in all its glory. In this process, light is exposed, which can then infiltrate the darkness, bringing a clearer direction for all minds and hearts.

For some, trying to relate this with an open heart and mind—during many of the world's crisis—is difficult to do. It is far easier, is it not, to accept this as the way life is, being suppressed, cajoled, or brainwashed … whether that's by a 'madman' or even by society. The more difficult road (but one in which you'll find salvation) is more often a royal one. Indeed, it is the divine path of your own soul. Through this, it links with the eternal threads of justice, truth, and peace from me, and to all life.

As I have mentioned before, the simpler road is littered with false starts, misguided ambitions, and all-to-brief searches for the missing pieces of the jigsaw. There are countless 'if only' signs being illuminated by your own light, which fade at many crossroads. In reality, though, they are those decisive, decision making 'moments' of your life so far.

Comprehend please, that while thousands of years have passed, parts of me have descended upon the Earth to impart wisdom to all those who would listen, opening their hearts through faith and trust. Mohammed, Jesus, and Krishna, to name a few, were all noted as 'prophets' full of love and divine guidance. Their appearance was to release you from the bondage of your own incarnations into the denser energy of embodiment.

In many religions, some will even state you are all the 'fallen', in terms of being 'gross' and/or 'subtle', within many layers of energy. Thus, it is not too far from reality. Appreciate then if you are light, then no matter wherever you are, you will shine. Though how bright is entirely down to your soul's development. Even a single shard of light can pierce through the deep abyss, into those darkest of times and places. So, there is always … yes, always, hope.

Therefore, as millions of people succumb to a fear of the unknown, with these general predictions or lies which attempt to control or manipulate both minds and hearts, know that there are still many more of light. Through the shift of change—and consciousness—the world will look anew, too, and for the future. So then, is there a prophecy still to come? Is it for good, for truth, for love, and for hope? Where now is the prophet for today or even, perhaps, the return of the messiah?

Well, please understand if there is one thing you will always remember from these lessons (whether that is from these books 1, 2 or 3), you will have grasped that 'he' is already within you. Please then, do not look into the night sky upon the multitude of stars—which are barely a fragment of creation—and ask or pray anymore for one's deliverance. Please do not doubt any longer of whom or what you are, but elevate your mind, heart, and soul to scale greater heights in the knowledge you have found me at last.

I am I, the Indweller of your heart, and in recognizing me, you will have finally recognized your own self. In truth, these words are only and exactly that, just words. However, when you finally open your heart, you will discover a richness of purity, of light, and of peace. These can never be erased, broken, burnt, or buried so deeply that you will ever lose sight of the truth.

Remember, I am God, and you are God. Therefore, the God in me 'IS'. Then, as, and when the ascension of your soul takes place, you will have re-discovered your own paradise into eternity. Think of all the amazing sights, sounds, and experiences of your life so far, and even if you multiplied them all by an infinite number of times, nothing would truly compare.

Turn within. Let me be your guide and confidant, as well as a friend, teacher, and listener. I am everything you will ever need and more. This is a very real 'prophecy' which can and will come true. Amen.

LESSON 52:
WELCOME

If this lesson is supposed to be the so-called ending, then its title is kind of ironic, don't you think? Perhaps I must have a sense of humour too, after all? Well, I promise not to draw this to a close, with anything other than the same wish and desire I have had for you all along. For you to finally understand our connection and your own self-realization.

Through this, you'll have discovered the well of your own heart, which nourishes your soul. You have also become renewed with the determination to shine and bloom with the fragrance of our divine essence. So too, your mind is less concerned with those things which you have no control of ... or over. At the same time, understand the power of thought which can create. Thoughts can resonate love and light far beyond the four walls where you physically live ... or bring aid to other negative energies, continuing to add pressure, pain, or fear to the world around—or even far beyond—you.

Some may feel they have come along a fantastic journey of accumulated knowledge, and through new experiences, gained wisdom. Others perhaps not so, taking small 'baby steps', but nonetheless, everything has its purpose. Even if it is not initially apparent or recognized.

I urge you not to accept anyone else's truth, only in what you feel is yours. Therefore, in being your own, be rest assured that no matter what road or path you have taken, it still leads and returns you back to me. It is important you remember to have faith in this, and even more so in yourself. Therein lies 'me', the answer to all things. Remember, I love you, so how could this not be so?

So, every day you can rise and face what comes with dignity, in the knowledge you have both the strength and fortitude to withstand any other's attempt to misguide or hide truth from you. You're now made of sterner stuff. You now recognize you are naturally born with—and equipped—with defence mechanisms both within and around you.

So, when ego attempts to rear its ugly head, you can combat this with humbling thoughts of those less fortunate than yourself. There is nothing like a contentment issue to help one accept who and what you are—as well as what you have—with those who, in life, seem to have very little 'choice'.

Know that just as your heart beats and pumps the life-giving force through your body, so too your soul. This is being sustained and nourished through 'right action', which can now help pull and link new hearts and minds together as one.

We're all in this as one. You can all be as useful and as resourceful as you would like or need to be. By acknowledging others, your spiritual gifts and creativity (which will become known to you, if not already) will be displayed like a picture in a gallery. Others can then see and bear witness. Remember also—in a previous statement—please do not ask whether you are big or small, because every grain of sand on a beach is vital, for it makes one whole.

Okay, so where you go from here is entirely up to you. Do you feel you need to change anything within or around you? What traits enhance your own or your families' lives? Could you change anything within or 'without' if you feel you ought to?

I urge you to simplify your life. This leads you to accepting yourself and others, for life is only as complicated as you believe or deem it to be. The important time is right now. Yes, today! Tomorrow will take care of itself. So, by working through it (doing the best that you can), someone can say or ask no more of, or from, you. Release frustration and uncertainty, not by carrying pain through word of mouth, but by openly letting your love flow from you. If anyone remains doubtful, just try letting go of a loved one who is suffering in body, mind, or soul at this time, for it is not an easy thing to do.

And so then, we've nearly completed another 'chapter' or phase of one's life. Let's say goodbye to anger, jealousy, fear, and hate, which all lead to the malnutrition of your soul. I welcome you to my eternal table where you are (and can be) forever nourished, so please come and partake in me.

Appreciate the words 'I am the way, the truth and the life' which echo and resonate in every language and for every man, woman, child, bird, or beast. So please, finally understand your own true nature of being. We are whole. Nothing can divide or ever separate you from me, and vice versa. All will fail because it is an illusion.

Like your life, let it always be an open book, and may these snippets of text carry you forward, as it is a never-ending story. You are writing your own history every day, and may they each become permanent markers and indicators of just how far you have travelled as a person, human being, and a soul.

One day, when the soul is ready, you'll cast off the dense overcoat of the body, which we have discussed before. Please do not have any regrets. May your so-called obituary leave a legacy and read true, as an example for others to follow.

I AM I The Indweller of Your Heart—Book Three

When all is said and done, I will lift you upon golden chariots of light. Your soul will burn more brightly than a thousand suns. It will shine in all directions, signalling your arrival and a return to your true and full state of being. You will receive a welcome like no other, surrounded by all the love you could imagine and more.

This love is the essence of all you have emitted from your heart centre, be that of (and to) family, friends, and pets throughout creation. It all comes back to you, from every source you have recognized and known in truth. Tears of joy will erase all the false pain of separation. In this moment, you'll finally, undeniably, and eternally know we are all 'one'. Amen.

CONCLUSION

"How and where you go from here is entirely up to you, as it is all of your own making. Your hopes, wishes, and dreams can therefore rise and pierce the ether; to reach beyond the stars and through every dimension … or they can fade, just like a memory, and eventually disappear without a trace.

Know then, without love inside your heart, they cannot thrive (or even exist), and because you are each your own creation, self-realization can only be reached by one's efforts whilst living in truth.

Please appreciate, therefore, that 'light' is forever within. It also watches over you, but true peace and bliss is not only 'known' by arriving at a predetermined destination. In reality, it is here right now. You just have to believe it to be true and it can be.

May God bless you upon your own journey and path you take. I wish you strength, conviction, fortitude, and good luck … each and every day." DK

FURTHER READING

You will find your own guidance and inspiration every day, week, month or year as nothing in life is ever by 'chance'. Each Lesson will simply be the most appropriate for your needs at that time, helping you to find inner peace and balance, as well as your own spiritual education, growth and understanding. Here is a selection of my favourite books and authors, which I hope you will enjoy reading too.

Sai Baba Gita-
The Way to Self-Realization and Liberation in this age.
By Al Drucker
ISBN 0-9638449-0-3

Conversations with God
By Neale Donald Walsh
Book 1 - ISBN 0-340-69325-8
Book 2 - ISBN 0-340-76544-5
Book 3 - ISBN 0-340-76545-3

The Message of a Master
By John McDonald
ISBN 0-931432-95-2

The Celestine Prophecy- An Adventure
By James Redfield
ISBN 0-533-40902-6

Anastasia- The Ringing Cedar series -Book 1
By Vladimir Megre
ISBN 978-0-9801812-0-3

A Course in Miracles
By The Foundation for Inner Peace
ISBN 0-670-86975-9

The Winds of Change
By Stephanie J. King
ISBN 978-0954242169

The Day my life changed
By Carmel Reilly
ISBN 978-1-84509-420-1

Confessions of a Pilgrim
Bu Paulo Coelho
ISBN 0-7225-3293-8

A Mind of your Own
By Betty Shine
ISBN 0-00-255894-7

Angel Inspiration
By Diana Cooper
ISBN 0-340-73323-3

Chicken Soup for the Soul
By Jack Canfield and Mark Victor Hansen
ISBN 0-09185-428-8

The Complete Book of Dreams
By Edwin Raphael
ISBN 0-572-01714-6

The Bible Code
By Michael Drosnin
ISBN 0-297-82994-7

Noah Finn & the Art of Suicide
By E. Rachael Hardcastle
ISBN: 978-1999968816

Noah Finn & the Art of Conception
By E. Rachael Hardcastle
ISBN: 978-1999968861

ABOUT THE AUTHOR

David has helped to conduct spiritual development and healing circles for over 25 years. He has also been a guest speaker—sharing his enlightened experiences to promote 'oneness'—at various Mind, Body and Spirit engagements across the UK.

Through inner-dictation, dream interpretation, meditation, mindfulness, pre-cognition, and healing, the books he co-writes with 'Spirit' provide you with the foundation to discover your own path of truth. With a renewed sense of purpose, the spiritual guidance and education you receive can help you reach the goal of self-realization and bliss within the permanence of love and light.

David is tee-total and a vegetarian, who loves the sunshine, nature, animals, and his wife!

INVITATION FROM DAVID KNIGHT

If you enjoyed reading *I AM I The Indweller of Your Heart* —**Book Three,** you can download *Deliverance of Love, Light and Truth* for free when you join David's mission for a 'full and blissful life'.

To learn more, visit www.AscensionForYou.com

I AM I The Indweller of Your Heart—Book Three

Follow us on

Facebook: facebook.com/ascensionforyou
or
Twitter: twitter.com/ascensionforyou

and become part of our community who love to receive uplifting messages for the heart and soul!

Want to let others know what you think? Please make your opinion known by leaving a 'star rating' with one-click at your favourite online retailer.

Thank you!

www.ingramcontent.com/pod-product-compliance
Lightning Source LLC
LaVergne TN
LVHW011830060526
838200LV00053B/3966